Organizational Wisdom in 100 African Proverbs

An Introduction to Organizational Paremiology

Published by
Adonis & Abbey Publishers Ltd
St James House
13 Kensington Square
London
W8 5HD
Website: http://www.adonis-abbey.com
E-mail Address: editor@adonis-abbey.com

Nigeria:
No. 3, Akanu Ibiam Str.
Asokoro,
P.O. Box 1056, Abuja.
Tel: +234 7066 9977 65/+234 8112 661 609

Year of Publication 2014

Copyright© Chiku Malunga

British Library Cataloguing-in-Publication Data
A catalogue record for this book is available from the British Library

ISBN: 978-1-909112-47-6

The moral right of the author has been asserted

All rights reserved. No part of this book may be reproduced, stored in a retrieval system or transmitted at any time or by any means without the prior permission of the publisher

Organizational Wisdom in 100 African Proverbs:

An Introduction to Organizational Paremiology

Chiku Malunga

TABLE OF CONTENTS

Acknowledgements..v
Dedication..vi
Foreword..vii
INTRODUCTION...9

CHAPTER ONE
The Organization Development Process......................................19

CHAPTER TWO
Assessments in Organizational Paremiology................................37

CHAPTER THREE
Self-Development...61

CHAPTER FOUR
Relationships Development...85

CHAPTER FIVE
Strategy, The Art of Creating the Future we want.......................105

CHAPTER SIX
Organizational Structure..125

CHAPTER SEVEN
Organizational Policies, Systems and Procedures........................139

CHAPTER EIGHT
Cultivating Organizational Wisdom:
The Organization Development Process 161

INDEX 207

Acknowledgements

Special thanks go to my colleague Charles Banda without whose involvement this book would not be what it is. Special thanks again go to the Impact Alliance team for their editorial and creative support, critique and numerous enhancing ideas. I truly appreciate their commitment to the project and the patience they have demonstrated. Thanks Meg Kinghorn, Sue Bloom, Evan Bloom and Chris Benet.

Dedication

I dedicate this book to all the people who believe in development, especially the development of Africa. I also dedicate it to all the sons and daughters of Africa in diaspora. I believe it will offer them a means to reconnect with their roots in mother Africa and inspiration to make more contribution to her development.

Foreword

It is a great privilege and honor to be asked to write the Foreword to this book that is in a field very new to me - *Organizational Paremiology*, but which has ancient roots. Though born an American, after living more than 40 years in Nigeria, I have learned to appreciate the cultural heritage on this continent and the need for Africans to embrace their social identity which has often been neglected and cast aside while adopting Western ideologies. We have often thrown away the good of this land as being 'out-dated' or 'irrelevant' in today's world. Africans have lost much of 'who we are' and adopted a way of life that is also fraught with problems. In the era of globalization and the view that the world is a 'global village', we still need to recognize the value of the ideals born and nurtured in the African village as a key to finding sustainable and lasting development strategies.

Organizing and management of people is not a new concept – it is as old as human existence itself. Human beings are social beings. Though, as the author has stated, civilization has gone through different stages as knowledge and technology have advanced, the basic nature of people has remained the same. This book recognizes, documents and helps us to apply the wisdom of old as we deal with contemporary challenges in the organizational life of the present.

The variety and richness of the proverbs in this book truly reflect the wisdom of the ancestors, recognizing that knowledge and understanding are not the same as the number of years of formal education in the Western sense. By celebrating these proverbs, the book demonstrates the appreciation that Africans place on the wisdom and experience of the elders, rather than the practice of many societies that throw away the perspectives of the elderly and long-held traditions.

The intended audience of this book cuts across development practitioners, managers, educationists at all levels and other stakeholders both within and outside Africa. In other words, it has something for everyone. Even the entertainment value makes it appealing and beneficial to all readers.

Beyond its informative and entertaining qualities, however, the book is a serious academic reference for analytically understanding organization development and improving organizational effectiveness, helping managers and staff, teachers and students, officials and the governed as well as practitioners and beneficiaries to more effectively guide the process of organizational development, leadership and management. It accomplishes this objective in a unique and even humorous manner, making the reading of an otherwise sometimes dry topic to be very enjoyable.

I have found many treasures in this book as I read through the pages. I plan to incorporate some of these proverbs in my teaching of African university students in an attempt to also sensitize them to the value of traditional proverbs and indigenous wisdom as they attempt to find solutions to rural development problems and effectively build up the potentials in Africa. It is time for us to not only look to developed countries for answers to our challenges, but also to look within and indigenize our thinking. This book helps us on our journey back home.

Janice E. Olawoye
Professor of Rural Sociology
Department of Agricultural Extension and Rural Development
University of Ibadan, Nigeria

INTRODUCTION

Organizational Wisdom in 100 African Proverbs is motivated by the need to find more effective ways of improving personal and organizational performance. It is built on the idea that the indigenous wisdom contained in African proverbs can be used to communicate 'modern' organizational issues much more eloquently than most conventional methods. One proverb can explain an organizational issue much more effectively than an entire chapter in a classic organizational or management text book. A proverb like *if the sun says it is more powerful than the moon then let it come and shine at night* for example demonstrates the importance of people holding senior positions in organizations to recognize and respect the role played by the others holding less senior positions more forcefully than is possible with most conventional methods. The use of African proverbs, therefore, offers an opportunity to improve organizational performance in ways that may not be possible with most conventional methods.

Human civilization has gone through four distinct ages of organization. These are: the hunter/gatherer, agricultural, industrial and the information/knowledge ages. Each age or era had its own appropriate way for designing and managing organizations. The industrial age often took a mechanistic view and focused only on the efficiency of the worker stifling the human spirit in the process. The information age requires a holistic view that focuses on not only the efficiency but also the effectiveness of the worker and work teams. Taking a holistic view and focusing on effectiveness in the information age signifies a shift to an emphasis on organizational wisdom as 'wisdom is applied information or knowledge'. The shift to the era of wisdom signifies the need to treat organizations as natural, human and responsive systems integrated with people's culture and values. Since *when the beat of the drum changes, so must the step of the dance*, a major challenge facing organizations today is to make a conscious shift away from the industrial age way of designing and managing organizations to the wisdom age way of designing and managing organizations. If organizations are going to attain and improve their performance, they must change the step of their dance to suit the beat of the drum that the age and era in which they exist implies. They must make a conscious shift away from the industrial era to the era of organizational wisdom.

As a hangover from the industrial age era, many organizational leaders are often more skilled in project related competencies (the doing part) as compared to organizational competencies (the being and relating part). An individual's project knowledge, whether in business in the private sector or in food security, HIV/AIDS, environment or human rights in the non-governmental or civil society sector, does not necessarily include organizational knowledge and competencies needed for effective organizational management and development. In short, many organizational leaders while strong on project issues are not as strong on organizational issues. This leads to more concentration on the projects rather than the internal capacity and the collaboration and networking issues of the organization. Lack of concentration on the internal capacity and collaboration and networking issues of the organization eventually undermines the efficiency and effectiveness of the projects and activities. Increased organizational rather than project knowledge only would lead to a balanced focus. Only that organization that is maintaining this balance can boast organizational integrity, sustainability and impact.

Complicating the above challenge further is the inadequacy of appropriate efforts to promote effective organizational knowledge despite the explosion in available information in general. Effective and appropriate efforts to improve organizational effectiveness that would match the pace of change (both in the task environment and within the organizations themselves) and help organizations adapt to the emerging age of wisdom are scarce. This is more pronounced in the developing countries in general and Africa in particular, though the developed world is not spared. Developing countries have to depend on organizational efforts designed and developed mostly in America and Europe. In 1994, while I was an undergraduate student at the University of Malawi, I was fortunate to be involved in a project by the American Association for the Advancement of Science (AAAS) to assess the type of published materials available in the library by authors and the place of residence of the authors. I was assigned the section on development studies. The major finding I can remember from the assessment was that the number of African authors resident on the continent were the least, almost insignificant category. Today, nothing much has changed. African authors living on the continent remain the least category on personal and organizational development materials on the continent. As a result, Africa still lacks her own voice and people who can speak to her on issues facing the continent and the world as an African contribution to international issues today.

To be truly effective, organizations in Africa must evolve a home grown system of organization that suits their culture and heritage. Direct copying of ideas from Northern or Eastern cultures will not work. We will greatly benefit if we build on the organizational advancements from these areas but they will only work for us if we contextualize them. When we build this organizational system, the people in the North and East will also benefit by getting insights from us that they can contextualize in their situations. This cross-fertilization of ideas is what is needed for synergy in an environment where the whole world is becoming one global village. Using the wisdom contained in African proverbs to promote organizational knowledge and practice presents an unlimited and timeless way of understanding organizational effectiveness in an era of continuous change.

Related to the above is the scantiness of comprehensive and relevant resources to help organizational leaders and consultants manage effective organizational change processes. As already pointed out, there are so many resources on different aspects of project management. There are far less resources, in relative terms, on organizational development especially as they relate to developing countries and their contexts in general. As a result, organizations in developing countries have to borrow frameworks and models from America and Europe.

The book uses the indigenous wisdom contained in African proverbs to awaken organizational consciousness appropriate for the age of organizational wisdom and show how organizations can go through an organizational performance improvement process through African Proverbs based Organization Development (OD) interventions. Against this background, the book is aimed at:

1. Bringing an Indigenous Wisdom Based Organization Development (Organizational Paremiology) awareness to organizational leaders and change agents
2. Presenting an African Proverbs based approach and frameworks to facilitating OD processes in organizations to all types of organizations worldwide.
3. Demonstrating that the wisdom contained in African Proverbs can contribute positively to modern life in general.

What are Proverbs?

Proverbs are an integral part of African culture. They are simple statements with deep meaning. They are *sentences edited from long experiences*. They are guidelines for individual, family and village behaviour, built upon repeated real life experiences and observations over time. Proverbs are a mirror through which a people look at themselves -- a stage for expressing themselves to others. *A proverb is the mirror of the community*. The way people think and look at the world, their culture, values, behaviours, aspirations and preoccupations can immediately be understood by looking at their proverbs.

While Africa has many languages and cultures, proverbs offer them common ground. The same proverbs recur in similar forms in almost all African languages and societies. Some state facts from a people's history, customs and practices; others express philosophical thoughts, beliefs and values. Yet, they make communication instantly possible, irrespective of differences in geographic origin and cultural backgrounds. Proverbs are the common property of Africans because they are ascribed to wisdom of all the ancestors. A preceding statement like "so said the ancestors" accords the proverb its unquestionable authority.

Use of Proverbs

According to BBC's Wisdom of Africa book, *"proverbs are used to illustrate ideas, reinforce arguments and deliver messages of inspiration, consolation, celebration and advice"*. More specifically:

- Proverbs identify and dignify a culture. They express the collective wisdom of the people, reflecting their thinking, values and behaviours. Using proverbs to communicate and understand organizational issues is a very powerful tool in the quest for a genuine African identity.
- In indigenous Africa, proverbs are used to unlock stuckiness, clarify vision and unify different perspectives. Proverbs add humour and diffuse tension on otherwise very sensitive issues. Every African society has used proverbs for centuries to ease uncomfortable situations, confront issues and build institutions and relationships. They can be understood where literacy is low and yet appreciated by even the most educated.
- Proverbs are metaphors and can explain complex issues in simple statements. A proverb like, *a stewed liver may look smooth and easy to swallow but it can choke one to death* may be a powerful statement in encouraging people to change their sexual behaviour in the light of HIV and AIDS i.e. not to be deceived by how somebody looks and assume that they cannot infect them with the virus. Proverbs like: *when one begs for water it does not quench thirst, the person being carried does not know how far the town is, if you borrow a man's legs, you will go where he directs you*, encourage people to be self-reliant and they can explain with more force the concept of sustainability than other conventional methods.
- Proverbs are like seeds. They only become 'alive' when they are 'sown'. They are simple statements until applied to real life situations, bringing them to life and expanding their meaning.
- By being metaphorical, proverbs create strong mental pictures. This is a great tool for motivating people to action.

Proverbs as Metaphors

> Metaphors and analogies draw relationships of likeness between two things– often very unlike things- and are used for vividness, for clarification, or to explain certain emotions. And it is difficult to move people without touching their emotions. A metaphor enables a person to visualize the object and then go through a mental process of making sense of what the message means on a visual, cognitive and emotional level. There is often a moment of puzzlement trying to decode the message; this pause ensures that the listener is both stimulated and concentrating on the speaker's message. In this case, the metaphor presents a paradox. Something that should not be but is. For example the proverb, *"ants united, can carry a dead elephant to their abode"*. The ants cannot carry an elephant but in the metaphor they do. It is also a paradox that ends on a positive note. The ants are able to carry the dead elephant to their cave. The reader then interprets the paradox in terms of himself or herself. In this case, the power of the metaphor is to pass a very powerful message of determination and possibility.
>
> Metaphors are most potent when they invoke symbols that have deep cultural roots and as a result, elicit strong emotions. African proverbs are deeply rooted in African society. And since the proverbs are not really African but human proverbs, they elicit strong emotions in all people from everywhere.

Adapted from Conger, 1998: 78

What is Organizational Paremiology?

A paremiologist is a person who collects proverbs. Paremiology is the study of proverbs. Organizational Paremiology is the application of the wisdom in proverbs to the understanding and practice of Organization Development. Over the past 15 years we have worked with several organizations in many countries in Africa and beyond in using this approach. We have also written extensively on different Organization Development topics using this approach. This book is an attempt to put in one place our comprehensive understanding of the practice of Organization Development seen from a paremiologist's lenses. In a way, Organizational Paremiology is an indigenous version of Organization Development. Put simply, Organizational Paremiology is indigenous wisdom based Organization Development.

This book's unique and special contribution to the body of knowledge and practice of Organization Development is in the introduction of the use of African proverbs as a tool for understanding and the practice of Organization Development. As of now, I do not know of any other Organizational Paremiologists in the world apart from ourselves. But I am sure that we will soon be joined by many others. Based on the global attention we are getting from our experimenting and practice efforts in introducing this new area of study and practice of Organizational Paremiology, we believe that the field will grow significantly in the future and further work by practitioners and academics will build on this introductory work.

The Audience of the Book

This book is meant to be a resource for raising organizational consciousness among organizational stakeholders interested in organizational capacity building namely (e.g., board members, managers, staff wishing to improve the performance of their organizations and donors). It is also meant to be a toolkit for OD practitioners and other consultants. In addition, it will make good leisure reading for those interested in indigenous wisdom and how it can be creatively applied to improve organizational performance and modern life in general. The book will be of particular value to volunteers and expatriates working in or coming to work in Africa and other developing regions; students and teachers of (organizational) development or African studies; and all development practitioners. The humour in the African proverbs can be a good way of managing stress which is so common arising from the increasing pressures of modern life. The book, therefore, makes general good reading for anybody.

How to Use this Book

When I visited Washington D.C to launch my first book, *"Understanding Organizational Sustainability through African Proverbs"*, a lot of people, especially Professor Coraile Bryant, then of Columbia State University, encouraged me to write a book on how people in general, including individuals, families, communities and countries can use the wisdom in the African proverbs in modern life. They reasoned that the wisdom contained in the proverbs is more about people and applying it to organizations only may be limiting. Being primarily an Organization Development Practitioner, I think I am still biased towards organizations but I believe the principles and lessons discussed in the book can be extended to the other groups as well.

Readers interested in gaining an understanding of what organizations are and how they function, grow and develop over time will find it necessary to go through the whole book. While each chapter is self-contained, organizations are complex systems and isolating topics may obscure this complexity and the big picture. Those more interested in how African proverbs can be used to understand organizations may find it useful to read the whole book or simply chapters of their greatest interest. Those interested in improving organizational performance may treat the book as a resource and a guide to interventions. The material in the book may form good background reading to stimulate reflection both for the OD practitioner and the people in the organization going through the OD process.

Specific *'African proverbs organizational assessment tools'* are found in their relevant chapters and can be used or modified according to the specific organizational situation. Organizations going through a " " exercise for example may find it useful to reflect on the proverbs on organizational culture to draw insights on their organization, forming a strong foundation for shared understanding.

Organizational Wisdom in 100 African Proverbs aims at demystifying the otherwise arcane language of Organization Development (OD) while at the same time enhancing its power through use of the inspiring and humorous language inherent in the African proverbs.

Chiku Malunga
Organizational Wisdom in 100 African Proverbs (An Introduction to Organizational Paremiology)
London & Abuja, Adonis & Abbey Publishers

This is the essence of Organizational Paremiology. The book is divided into eight chapters.

The first chapter presents an overview and a framework of the African Proverbs Based Organization Development (Organizational Paremiology) process upon which the subsequent chapters are built. The successive chapters then build on this by explaining in detail the different components of the Organizational paremiology process and presenting proverbs based tools for organisational improvement.

The second chapter discusses organizational assessments as the first step of the Organizational paremiology process. The chapter presents the assessment model and process. The subsequent chapter discusses interventions that can be implemented following an organizational assessment. Since no organization can rise above the level and quality of people it employs, the third chapter discusses self-development.

Chapter four discusses how organizations can ensure healthy relationships among the people in the organization through developing teams and team spirit, managing conflict and managing power and conflict. The chapter also discusses how to ensure effective inter-organizational relationships. The fifth chapter discusses the importance of strategic positioning for organizations. It discusses the strategic planning process and characteristics of effective strategies. It finally discusses the importance of linking organizational activities to the strategic plan of the organization.

The sixth chapter discusses how to ensure an effective organizational structure. The seventh discusses how to ensure effective organizational policies, systems and procedures for an organization. It discusses the major policies, systems and procedures needed in an organization and what determines what policies an organization needs. The last chapter concludes the book by discussing how the OD or Organizational paremiology process can be practically and effectively managed in an organization.

Michael Hammer (2003) starts his book *The Agenda* by observing that, "to write a business book today takes confidence that verges on foolhardiness. The business world changes so quickly that a book is likely to be irrelevant by the time it appears; one extolling innovation and growth will at best be quaint in a time of retrenchment and cost cutting. Even worse, the book's principles might have been proven invalid in the months between the completion of its manuscript and its appearance in print, or exemplars that the book cites may have fallen from grace" (pp xi). Being rooted in indigenous wisdom that transcends time and space thereby ensuring universal relevance, *Organizational Wisdom in 100 African Proverbs*, avoids Michael Hammer observation and warning. We need a few principles that we can lay our hands on despite the mind boggling rate of change in the task and internal organizational environments. While practice may and should change in response to these changes we still need a few principles that transcend time and space to give us some sense of sanity and stability in the reeling vortex of change. The wisdom contained in African proverbs gives a means to achieve this goal. This is the real value of the new field of Organizational Paremiology.

The aim of this book is not to present an exhaustive treatise on OD. Other books and writers are better placed to do that. The aim rather, is to demonstrate and introduce the use of African proverbs as a tool for enhancing the understanding and practice of the OD process. In other words, the aim is to introduce the new field of Organizational Paremiology. The success of the book, therefore, will be measured not so much on how well it presents OD as a practice but on how well it makes a case for the indigenous wisdom contained in African proverbs as a tool for personal and organization development. The success will be measured on how well the book makes a case for Organizational Paremiology.

CHAPTER ONE

The Organization Development Process

A healthy chick can be spotted the very day its egg is hatched

The chick that will grow into a strong rooster can be spotted the very day it is hatched. Similarly, a strong organization can be spotted by the organizational performance improvement efforts it is making. Organization Development is the parent of Organizational Paremiology. To understand Organizational Paremiology one needs to have an understanding of Organization Development. This chapter presents an overview of Organization Development (OD), as a distinctive way of improving organizational performance, by discussing its meaning and process. By giving an overview of Organization Development, the chapter also gives an overview of Organizational Paremiology. The subsequent chapters expand on the themes presented in this chapter.

The meaning of Organization Development

An egg does not hatch in a day
If you are patient enough, you can come out of the trap net
A patient mouse in a young banana plant will one day eat a ripe banana
More haste less speed
Shortcuts are full of mud
Life cannot be hurried

An organization is a living system made up of people who come together on some sort of a permanent basis with the aim of achieving some agreed or shared goal or goals. An organization is a living system because first of all it is made up of living people; and its existence transcends the individuals comprising it. In other words, the leaving of individuals and coming in of other individuals into the organization usually do not determine the existence of the organization although its health may be affected. Organization Development, therefore, refers to processes aimed at improving the system's legitimacy, sustainability and impact. Legitimacy refers to how well connected the organization is to the people it exists for, especially at the values or affective level. Sustainability refers to the organization's 'staying power' for as long as it is needed by the people it exists for, or the continuity of its benefits to the people it exists for. Impact refers to the positive permanent changes in the lives of the people accruing from the work of the organization.

The ultimate goal of all organization improvement efforts is to create organizations that have legitimacy and are sustainable and are creating impact. There are three main approaches to improving organizational legitimacy, sustainability and impact. These are: providing financial and material resources, skills training, and process facilitation.

There is a strong feeling in most organizations that if only they would get enough financial and material resources all their problems or challenges would disappear. People in such organizations are surprised to observe that the coming in of more financial and material resources often produces its own problems, which were not there before. A small local non-profit organization, which was working on a mainly voluntary basis, disintegrated when their annual budget suddenly jumped from $10 000/year to $ 100 000/year. Quarrels over who would now be on salary and who would not, how to ensure transparency, an upsurge in visitors and volunteers to the organization to 'learn about their successes and too many invitations to attend conferences and workshops led to the collapse of the organization. This is a common experience of many organizations, which 'suddenly become rich before they are ready'. Lack of preparation for riches may be worse than poverty.

Many organizations feel that if only they could have more highly qualified people, everyone would know what to do and do it well and therefore their problems or challenges would disappear. One also observes that organizations with highly educated and qualified people are not necessarily exempted from common organizational challenges. In fact, the experience of many organizations is that, when they send their people for training, the people often come back only to resign and go to 'greener pastures'. One of the common requests we usually get for our organization development consultancy services is from the so called 'professional organizations' where the biggest challenge is usually that the people are highly qualified in their technical fields but many times not in 'organizational aspects of the organization'. The ones that seek external help on these matters are usually the humble type. The majority would rather stay with their problems because they believe that being qualified as they are, they can't crack their problems, and nobody else may. They do not know that being technically qualified may not mean that one is also organizationally qualified.

In improving organizational performance, we can use principles of growth or principles of development. Both are important but an overemphasis of one over the other makes lasting organizational performance improvement impossible. Growth means to increase in size by the assimilation of materials. Development, on the other hand, means to expand or realize the system's potential; to bring to a fuller, greater, or better state (Becker, 1996:31). When something grows it gets quantitatively bigger, when it develops it gets qualitatively better. A baby grows by increasing in size. It develops by learning to sit, stand, walk, run and talk for example. Growth follows mechanical laws while development follows natural laws. We can make an organization grow by increasing its financial and material resources; and also by increasing its skills and competencies base. This can happen within a relatively short period of time. By simply signing a check or recruiting more and well-qualified people we can achieve organizational growth.

Natural laws are different from mechanical laws in that while we can create growth, we cannot create development. We can only nurture it. We can make organizations grow but we cannot make them develop. Their development is a natural process. As Albert Einstein, the father of modern physics, once said, *"I never teach my pupils; I only attempt to provide the conditions in which they can learn"*, we can only create facilitative conditions in which the development process can thrive and is not delayed. A chicken's egg takes 21 days to hatch when incubated. A guinea fowl's egg takes 28 days to hatch. If a chicken or a guinea fowl is sitting on the eggs, we cannot hasten the process. We cannot hasten the incubation period. If we want more chicks and may be more frequently, we can only increase the number of the eggs being incubated and their sequencing one way or another. But we cannot change the 21 or 28 days rule because development is a natural process. We can't make the eggs hatch; we can only wait until their right time to hatch.

Similarly, organizations, because they are made up of human beings, are natural systems and therefore they follow natural laws of development. Organizational growth efforts alone are not adequate. In order to be effective, organizational growth efforts must be based on the foundation of organizational development efforts. Based on this understanding, OD is the process, led and supported by an organization's leaders to create facilitative conditions for the *'organizational egg to hatch a healthy chick'*. Such a process cannot be hurried though it can be delayed. It is natural and therefore requires patience. It can only move as fast as the conditions allow it. The work of the OD practitioner is to create conditions that will enable development to take place. While the leaders and practitioners can cause growth to happen, they cannot directly cause development to happen.

Efforts to bring about organizational growth preoccupy most organizations. Much of what is called OD today is actually about trying to create organizational growth. For organizations to have legitimacy, be sustainable and make impact, the growth efforts must be built on the foundation of the development process. The greatest challenge, however, is that, while the growth aspects of the organization are the most felt and visible, the development needs are usually unfelt and unconscious. Awakening this consciousness is,

---

Chapter One | Chiku Malunga
Organizational Wisdom in 100 African Proverbs (An Introduction to Organizational Paremiology)
London & Abuja, Adonis & Abbey Publishers

therefore, a key need in most organizations and the purpose of this book.

True, organizational and personal transformation cannot happen if it does not occur at the 'development or process' level. Financial and material resources improve the organization's *doing*. Similarly, the organization's skills and competencies improve its *doing*. It is only the organization's development processes that can change its *being*. It is who we are that ultimately determines what we are capable of doing. An organization can only use its financial and material resources; and skills and competencies to the level of its *being*. The excess is wasted. At the same time, a higher level of its *being*, may compensate for its lack of financial and material resources; skills and competencies and much more importantly it may build the organization's capacity to gain these. This is why organizations with a lot of material and financial resources; skills and competencies may still fail while those with a minimum of these but with a higher level of *being* may succeed. Countries with very little financial and material resources like Singapore understood this principle in the 1960s and used it to develop to become one of the world's richest countries. They also understood that *consciousness* precedes *being*. This is why awakening consciousness is an indispensable aspect of organization development processes.

As explained above, most organizational improvement efforts are aimed at the *doing* of the organization. Not much is known about how we can change the *being* of the organization. The essence of OD is how we can change the *being* of an organization. OD aims at raising the bar of an organization's level of *being*. We strongly believe that organizations will not experience deep, evolutionary, transformative and lasting change if they do not consciously undergo developmental processes as described above. In striving to *do* more, organizations should more importantly strive to *be* more. While *doing* more may work in the short term, *being* more is always long-term.

Chapter One | Chiku Malunga
Organizational Wisdom in 100 African Proverbs (An Introduction to Organizational Paremiology)
London & Abuja, Adonis & Abbey Publishers

The OD Process

The greatest problem is to be conscious of none

The OD process is based on the development process. A development process model is presented below.

Fig 1. The Development Process

Ineffective interventions		effective interventions
Undesired 'gravity' Situation	'Stuckiness', Desired 'meaninglessness' and Situation frustration	Contradiction 'success (turning point) Precipitation of a crisis

Development is a process of moving from an undesired to a desired situation. Put simply, development is good change. The way to transform undesired to desired situations is through effective interventions. Effective interventions, however, are only possible if the system or people involved undergo a 'contradiction', which results in a turning point. This is often manifested through a crisis. The explanation why many development efforts fail is that they are implemented without the system or people undergoing a contradiction. Similarly, the explanation why many organizational development efforts fail is because they are implemented without the organization undergoing the contradiction stage. The contradiction enables people to see how their past decisions and actions have created the present undesired situation. By this understanding, they can also be brought to understand how a conscious change in their decisions and actions today can create the desired situation tomorrow. An understanding of the principle of contradiction encourages *people to judge each day not by its harvest but by the seeds they sow into it*. Contradiction, therefore, is the foundation for effective interventions. Without this, foundation interventions cannot be truly effective. Contradiction is the essence of *consciousness* which comes before *being*.

Undergoing the contradiction process brings to consciousness the incongruence between what people want to be and do and what they are and what they actually do. It is innate in every human being to want to make progress, to live a better life, to become and feel more important. But often times, we are not conscious of the mismatch between what we want and what we are or do or how what we are and do stand in the way of our realizing of what we truly want. In other words, we want a better life without changing ourselves and our actions, which stand in the way to the standard of life we want. We don't want to be disturbed from our comfort zones. No major change, however, comes without a cost -- the cost of letting go of our comfort zones. The ability to see this is the essence of contradiction, development and organizational development.

Without going through the contradiction stage, people cannot see and appreciate that much of what they are experiencing today is a result of their past choices either directly or indirectly. *Many people smear themselves with mud and then complain that they are dirty.* They cannot see that they are responsible for the undesired situation they are experiencing. Such people abdicate responsibility to outside forces like other people, fate or some external forces. "The devil made me do it," is a common excuse of thieves in some parts of the world when they are caught. In order to be effective, organizational development efforts must challenge people to see that they are responsible for their 'organizational development' or lack of it. When people begin to believe for real that whether they succeed or fail it is their responsibility or at least their collective responsibility, they will get enough motivation to start moving towards their desired situations as individuals, organizations, communities and nations. Many people have given up any hope of improvement because they do not feel powerful enough to do something about their undesired situations. High staff turnover in many organizations can be explained by staff taking the 'route of least resistance' – getting a job somewhere else rather than 'fighting for the change they want within their organizations'. They forget that a *wise man marries the woman he loves but a wiser man loves the woman he marries*.

Without going through the contradiction stage, organization development interventions cannot be effective. The lack of transformation, which will result from the contradiction stage, will act as a block to the effectiveness of the interventions. The people will be stuck and will keep moving in a cycle of frustration and meaninglessness.

Based on the development model above, there are three components to all OD processes. These are: assessment, intervention, and process management.

Assessment– collection of data about the organization or the targeted units and processes of the organization. This also includes the contradiction stage which usually comes through the feedback session. At an individual level, this involves establishing where the person is today in relation to his or her *being, doing* and *relating*. This is the essence of the maxim *know thyself*.

Intervention planning–actions designed to improve the organization's functioning. All the interventions are aimed at surfacing contradictions and then correcting behaviour in response to the contradictions raised. The same applies to individuals.

Process management– all the activities designed to ensure the success of the OD process like developing the OD action plan, monitoring the events along the way, managing the surprises along the way and finally evaluating the OD process at the end. The process enables the organization to consciously strike a balance among its being, doing and relating.

Assessment

You can't know where you are going if you do not know where you are coming from

An assessment stems from two main needs. These are to know the current health status of the organization and to decide on corrective measures as a result. To be effective, assessments must be solution rather than problem centered. It is often more empowering to ask people what they want rather than what their problems are. The development model above begins with the creation of an ideal picture of the desired situation. *What the eyes have seen, the heart cannot forget*. The assessment process is therefore based on, "what can help or hinder us from realizing the ideal picture of the desired situation?" rather than 'how stuck are we?" The contradiction stage involves exploring, "how have our past decisions and actions created the current undesired situation?" and "How can lessons from the foregoing help us to create the desired future?"

Data analysis follows data collection. This is usually done in a feedback session. Joint data analysis between the OD practitioner and the client is encouraged for a number of reasons. Among these are: it reinforces ownership to the process, it helps clarify and separate perceptions from real issues; and it helps in joint prioritization and action planning

As stated above, part of the data analysis process involves challenging the client to see the contradictions in their behaviour and, therefore, how their decisions and actions have created the current undesired situation. By seeing how responsible they were in creating the current situation, they are also encouraged to see how responsible they are in creating the desired situation. The effectiveness of the OD practitioner can be measured by his or her ability to 'speak the unspeakable' – to raise the difficult issues that are normally avoided in the organization.

To be effective, assessments must: assess potential for action in the client (readiness, time, resources). People must be ready; they must commit time and resources to the OD process. They must give an assurance that they will take the implementation of the assessment findings seriously. *There is no point scratching where it is not itching;* help people see the 'whole picture' and the relationships within the picture; focus on the desired future and not to be caught up in the negative past or present; and recommend interventions and tasks that people can do for themselves.

The next chapter will discuss organizational assessments in detail. It will discuss the process of assessments and some of the models and tools one can use to conduct an effective organizational assessment.

OD Interventions

The action plan formulated after the assessment, point out to the interventions the organization will need to undertake in order to address the identified and prioritized issues. It is the road map to the desired situation. *What is the point of running so fast when you are on a wrong road?* OD interventions are sets of structured activities aimed at improving the culture and processes of the organization. The assessment show that OD interventions are often needed when: the organization is in a crisis, the organization is doing well but can foresee a crisis in the short or long-run and when the organization is already doing well but would like to build on its strengths. Most of the times, OD interventions are most effective when they take a preventive rather than curative approach. Most organizations, however, do not see the need for OD interventions when they are already doing well. They wait until when they are really sick before seeking help. This puts them in a 'quick solution fixing mode' which undermines the OD processes that they may undertake.

OD focuses on the human side of organizations. OD interventions, therefore, are aimed at improving the following processes in the organization:

Communication

This looks at how effective communication is in the organization by focusing on whether communication is directed upward or downward, or both. It also focuses on whether communication is filtered. If it is, why? In what way; and also whether the communication patterns and the situation fit.

Goal Setting

This looks at the effectiveness of the goals of the organization by focusing on whether the organization has goals, how are these arrived at, who participates in the goal setting, whether they have the necessary skills in setting effective goals, whether they can set short-range and long-range goals effectively.

Decision-making, Problem-solving, and Action Planning

This involves finding out who makes decisions or who makes what decisions, how effective the decisions are, whether decision-making skills are needed, whether problem-solving or solution identification skills are needed, whether the organizational members are satisfied with the decision making and problem solving or solution identification processes.

Conflict Resolution and Management

This process focuses on whether and where conflict exists in the organization, who are the parties involved in the conflict, how well is the conflict being managed, what are the system and procedures for dealing with conflict and whether the reward systems promote or discourage conflict.

Inter-group Relations

This may involve groups within the organization, e.g. teams, task forces, departments, board/secretariat relations. It may also involve the organization's relations with other organizations or stakeholders. It involves asking such questions as: How do the groups relate? Whether goals and expectations are clear? The major challenges the groups are facing in relating to each other. What are the structural conditions promoting or inhibiting healthy relationships?

Relations between Leaders and Followers

This looks at how leaders and their subordinates relate with each other. It involves examining leadership styles and their relevance to the situation in which they are applied. It also involves examining the challenges between the leaders and their subordinates.

Information, Communication, Technology (ICT)

This examines whether the organization has adequate and up to date ICT and whether the organization has capacity to use these efficiently and effectively. It also assesses whether the organization needs to plan and implement changes in this regard.

Strategic Leadership

This examines who in the organization is responsible for preparing the organization for tomorrow and whether these people have adequate capacity to that. It also involves reflecting on the effectiveness of current and recent strategic plans and decisions. What demands are coming from both within and without the organization? Whether the organization has enough capacity to respond to these and what it needs to work on in order to maximize its impact in its task environment. It also involves examining whether the vision, mission, and values are clear and shared by all in the organization.

Organizational Learning

This involves learning from the failures and successes of the organization. It involves reflecting on such questions as: from what we implemented, what worked well and what did not? What lessons or insights are we getting from the answers to the foregoing questions? How can we use these lessons and insights for more effective and efficient implementation?

In most organizational situations, the above processes are unconscious'. Problems in organizations are often just symptoms of a dysfunctional process or processes. When these processes are all working well most of the symptoms that organizations experience as problems would take care of themselves. *If you cannot stop the monkeys from coming to your banana tree cut down the tree.* This is why awakening the consciousness of and ensuring healthy organizational processes should be the essence of OD interventions.

OD interventions have three goals. These are: a learning or educational goal and an accomplishing task goal; focus on real organizational needs that are central to the needs of the organization rather than on hypothetical, abstract problems that may not fit the members' needs; and OD interventions use several learning models and frameworks and not just one

After the chapter on organizational assessments, the next chapters will discuss various OD interventions. The book will discuss OD interventions or the improvement of the processes on the following target groups that make up an organization and for the ensuing reasons:

Individual level–because personal effectiveness precedes organizational effectiveness; group or team level–because effective organizations work through teams; and organizational level–because lower improvement efforts can be frustrated by organizations' wide factors. Similarly, higher organizational efforts can be frustrated by weaknesses at lower levels.

OD Process Management

OD is a continuous process. It starts from entry, contracting, assessment, feedback, and interventions to evaluation. Managing the OD process is mostly involved with creating support systems and feedback loops to ensure continued relevance, timeliness and so forth of the OD program.

Entry – involves the initial contact between the consultant and the organization, finding out why the organization called and agreeing whether OD is really needed as not all situations need OD interventions.

Contracting– establishing mutual expectations between the consultant and the organization, reaching an agreement on the expenditure of time, money, resources, and energy and generally what each party expects from the other and promise to give. Contracting should also involve getting commitment to the implementation of the OD process as will be guided by the assessment findings. *How can two walk together before they agree?*

Assessment– fact-finding phase in which a picture of the situation is gained through interviews, observations, questionnaires, organizational information and literature review. It takes place in two phases – data gathering and data analysis. Assessments must be solution rather than problem oriented. Peter Drucker observes rightly when he says that in many organizations the bulk of time, work, attention and money first go to problems rather than to opportunities (Harvard Business School, 2006: 83).

Feedback– mirroring back to the organization the picture gained through the assessment. This helps to separate facts from perception and to ensure ownership of the process. It is at the feedback sessions that action plans are formulated and agreed on. The consultant and the organization also agree on how the implementation of the plan will be monitored and evaluated. This often involves selecting a 'task force' from within the organization to 'manage the OD processes.

Interventions– these are sets of actions to address the identified and prioritized issues.

Monitoring and Evaluation– Monitoring helps to ensure that the process is on track or to identify any emerging issues needing attention. Evaluation is done at the end to assess the results of OD process or to see if the OD process has managed to help the organization to realize its ideal picture. It involves asking such questions as: what worked well? What did not work well? What lessons have we learnt from the process? And how can we improve next time?

Chapter One	Chiku Malunga
	Organizational Wisdom in 100 African Proverbs (An Introduction to Organizational Paremiology)
	London & Abuja, Adonis & Abbey Publishers

The OD Process as a Change Process

Change refers to differences arising from passage of time. An understanding of the key ingredients of the change process gives a lot of insights to the successful management of the OD process. According to (Beckhard & Pritchard, 1992: 75), four key ingredients are crucial for the successful implementation of the change process. These are: level of dissatisfaction with the status quo; desirability of the proposed change or the end state; practicality of the change (minimal risk and disruption); and the cost of changing

For change to be successful, the organization must reach a threshold of dissatisfaction with the status quo. If people are satisfied with the way things are, they often do not see the need for change. This involves sensitizing people about the need for change. This is achieved by showing discrepancies between the undesired and the desired situation. This is aimed at creating pain and dissatisfaction with the undesired present.

The proposed change must be desirable to all the people involved. People naturally fear change for fear of the unknown. They are not sure whether through the change, they will go up or down, whether they will benefit or lose. Overcoming this requires involving organizational members in planning and implementing the change. It also involves showing the people how they will fit into the desired situation.

While the desired situation may be attractive, people may not commit to it if it implies maximum risk and disruption to normal life. Change interventions must as much as possible be those that the client can do for himself or herself with minimum support and guidance from the external facilitator. The sequencing of the interventions must also be well thought through. Start with the easiest and move to the more comprehensive and complex ones. Early success builds confidence and motivation to handle the subsequent more difficult interventions.

All change efforts have a cost. The cost may be in terms of readiness, time and other resources. Change efforts must be sensitive to what the organization can afford. Many times, however, organizational leaders get too excited and commit to such long-term change processes as OD processes without thinking through the costs implied. Change efforts that are not sensitive to what the organization can afford in terms of money, time and energy often end up in frustration.

Summary

OD is the process, led and supported by an organization's leadership to create facilitative conditions for the *'organizational egg to hatch a healthy chick'*. Such a process cannot be hurried though it can be delayed. It is natural and therefore requires patience in recognition that *short cuts are full of mud*. The central lesson in understanding the meaning of OD is that, *it is not money that builds a house but wisdom*. In other words, financial and material resources; and skills and competences alone are not enough without the foundation of effective organizational processes. Indeed, *a fool and his money are soon parted*, meaning that an organization without a strong foundation will find it difficult to attract financial and other resources and it is likely to lose even the financial and other resources it may already have.

Understanding the Meaning of Organization Development (OD)

How does the following proverb help us understand the importance of investing in OD processes for our organization?

> *The chick that will grow into a healthy rooster can be spotted the very day its egg is hatched*

How does the following proverb help us to become conscious of and appreciate the importance of individual and collective responsibility for our organization's challenges and development?

> *The greatest problem is to be conscious of none*

How do the following proverbs help us to understand the importance of process or long-term interventions as compared to 'one-off-quick-fix' solutions in our organizational improvement efforts?

An egg does not hatch in a day
If you are patient enough, you can come out of the trap net
A patient mouse in a young banana plant will one day eat a ripe banana
Shortcuts are full of mud
More haste less speed

How does the following proverb teach about the importance of looking beyond financial and material resources and skills and competences in building organizational capacity?

It is not money that builds a house. It is wisdom.

CHAPTER TWO

Assessments in Organizational Paremiology

One cannot arrive at their destination in life if they do not understand how they arrived at where they are today
Health is wealth

Introduction

All living systems strive towards a higher equilibrium. This higher equilibrium is the state at which the whole system is in 'sync' with itself. It is the state at which the system attains coherence. When something goes wrong in any part of the system, all the other parts go to work to normalize it with the aim of maintaining equilibrium. When the system spends energy correcting wrongs in the system, usually the new equilibrium settled for is lower reducing the productivity of the system as a whole. Maintenance of the health of the system precedes all the other system functions. This is in recognition that the system cannot give what it does not have. This is why an organization that has a lot of organizational health challenges cannot be effective as the organization spends most of its energy in trying to fix its health challenges at the expense of being productive. This is the justification for organizational assessments. Instead of letting the system unconsciously deal with its organizational health challenges, an organizational assessment enables the organization to consciously identify its 'health issues' and deal with them, thereby releasing its energy towards more productive ends.

No individual can arrive at their destination in life if they do not understand how they arrived where they are today. Similarly, organizations must periodically take some time to understand where they are today and how they got there as a basis for determining their desired future destinations. Conducting an organizational assessment is the first step in an organizational improvement process. Usually, this involves raising awareness of what a healthy organization would look like and establishing where the organization is today in relation to the 'desired picture'. Establishing the gap between the ideal and the current situation is the essence of an organizational assessment. The results of the assessment will point out to the type of interventions needed and how these interventions should be carried out.

When we began our practice at CADECO, we faced a number of challenges. Among these were: most of the organizational assessment tools in use were borrowed from North–America and Europe. In addition, most of the organizational assessment tools used in the non-profit sector were borrowed from the private or business sector.

We, therefore, embarked on formulating our own tools to take care of these problems. We came up with the African Proverbs based tools, which would enhance the communication of organizational issues in a language people from all types of organizations would easily understand. A sample of African proverbs organizational assessment tool is given in appendix 1.

What is an Organizational Assessment?

An organizational assessment is a 'checkup' to determine the health status of an organization. As in the tool above, the 'checkup' focuses on major aspects of an organizational health: the sustainability of the organization and its services; the skills, competencies and capabilities of its people; the way people relate to one another and the way the organization relates to its stakeholders; the policies, procedures and systems guiding decision making processes and, also, the strategy the organization and its implementation; the vision and mission of the organization; and the culture and values of the organization. *Health is wealth.* A healthy organization is potentially a wealthy organization if it uses its health well.

A healthy organization is the one in which there is synchrony among the above levels and they are all functioning properly. Only then can an organization boost its performance. This is what also distinguishes an organizational assessment from an evaluation or impact assessment. Many people confuse the two. An organizational assessment focuses on the 'internal aspects' of the organization while an evaluation looks at the results the organization is producing. The two are related in that a 'sick' organization cannot perform well.

The Purpose and Benefits of an Organizational Assessment

Conducting an organizational assessment is not an end in itself but a means toward an end. That end is developing an effective capacity building plan to guide the organization in its improvement efforts. By 'effective' I mean a capacity building plan that will actually be implemented. It is not enough to know how 'healthy' or 'unhealthy' an organization is if no action is undertaken to remedy the situation. The capacity building plan then becomes a 'bench mark' against which to measure progress in improving organizational health.

There are a number of benefits resulting from undergoing an organizational self-assessment. Among these are:

- Self-assessment is a powerful diagnostic tool. It is an objective health check and it is a predictor for an organization's long term success or failure
- Self-assessment enables organizations to make objective comparisons with other organizations or their 'ideal organization'. It provides benchmarking opportunities. It also enables the organization to compare the performance of its different departments. This helps the organization to discover strengths and areas for improvement. It also enables the organization to monitor its progress over time.
- Self-assessment provides a measure of the organization's capacity to meet the requirements and expectations of its clients and other stakeholders.
- Self-assessment can be a major motivation for process focused improvement activities in priority areas. It can form a strong basis for strategic planning and leadership processes.

In summary, organizational assessment enables the people in the organization to understand how they arrived at where they are today so that they can understand their organizations destination.

The Organizational Self-Assessment Process

The process of self-assessment goes through a number of stages. These are briefly outlined below:

1. OD Awareness

In most cases, an OD awareness session is needed. In our practice we have used two main frameworks to achieve this. These are phases of organization development and levels of complexity model as shown below:

Phases of Organizational Development

Even the biggest rooster that crows the loudest was once upon a time just an egg
It is better to be the head of a mouse than the tail of a lion

Organizations are natural social systems that grow and develop over time. They typically go through three distinct phases as they grow and mature, these being: the pioneer phase, the independent phase and the interdependent phase.

The Pioneer Phase

Organizations are normally started as an idea from an individual who, with the help of a few friends, implements the idea. Since the organization is made up of friends, there is a lot of informality in the organization. It is run like a family. The pioneer leader acts as a magnet to which everyone is attached. He or she spearheads formation of the organization's identity, vision, values, commitment and solidarity. The strength of the organization at this stage rests with the charisma of its leader and the power of its values and commitment. These alone are enough to sustain the organization. The organization may not have a strategic plan and it may not have a clear structure or even a structure at all. It usually does not have any policies, systems and procedures. The friends of the leader may not be identified on the basis of their merit but because of friendship or blood ties. At this stage, relationships are usually warm and satisfying. The organization probably does not have a lot of money or resources since it is usually quite small.

This stage is called the pioneer or dependent stage because the existence of the organization is dependent on the pioneer leader. He or she is the source of Identity and stability in the organization. Comparing it to human development, we can say that at this point the organization is a 'child'. This should not be understood to mean that the people in the organization are children or childish but rather that the organization as a whole portrays child-like characteristics, such as:

- High levels of energy and commitment because the sense of ownership is high;
- Personalized relationships and shared tasks among the pioneers (e.g., rotating leadership positions);
- High levels of informality– systems, procedures, policies are negligible because the group is usually small and has high levels of trust;
- Verbal communication and rapid consensus;
- Shared values and power and high loyalty;
- Strong dependency on the leader;
- Undefined roles and responsibilities;
- Lack of critique;
- Learning by imitation;
- Naïve of realities.
- Recognition comes through friendship and closeness to the founder

Like in human nature, the organization cannot remain a baby forever. It has to grow and develop. The transition from a baby to an adult is often precipitated by some natural crisis that causes a power shift in the organization. The typical forms crises take are:

- The pioneer leader may die, leave or become incapacitated, creating a vacuum. Without the central magnet or clear succession plans, people become sheep without a shepherd. This crisis calls for role clarification and differentiation, and written guidelines, policies and procedures.
- A rapid growth in staff may bring new people with different values and beliefs that conflict with the pioneers'. Or there may be so much growth that the leader loses control. Usually newcomers do not share the same values and commitments as the original group, causing confusion on how things are done and decisions are made. An expansion of the activities or services of the organization creates the need for restructuring and for new people to join the organization causing this turbulence. This crisis calls for law and order.
- The working environment may change radically, prompting the need to seek a new identity.

The crisis can kill the organization. Most of us know organizations that died with its owners. If the transition process is managed successfully, however, it can usher in the second phase

The Independent Phase

This phase arrives as a solution for the crisis in the first phase. Because of the loss of control, plans are made to introduce more order and departmentalization to the system. This phase is characterized by:

- More law and order- policies, procedures and systems are established;
- More professionalism- clear professional expectations emerge through job descriptions and specialization;
- Less personalization- people are known by their titles;
- More fairness - a salary structure may be developed;

- More hierarchy- control is usually shifted to the top.
- Recognition comes through formal qualifications and experience.

The next natural crisis that shapes the organization is a bureaucratic crisis. It is stimulated by:

- Growing commitment to profession over organization, which hinders the organization as people become more individualistic;
- Increased isolation and alienation– there is less informal interpersonal interactions, failure to identify with the purpose of the organization, separate offices with closed goals, people known by titles rather than names;
- Disappearing commitment to values and purpose, leading to boredom and decreased motivation;
- Shifting organizational focus to being self-serving with the needs of the people for which it exists becomes a secondary matter.

This alienation and loss of humaneness calls for more flexibility and a better organizational climate. This is done through improving communication, flattening management structures, enhancing team dynamics, managing conflict and encouraging self-development. These are characteristics of the third phase of organization.

The Interdependent Phase

The third stage is called the stage of effectiveness because it combines the positive characteristics of stages one and two. Extended families only work if all the families achieve autonomy. Relationships are symbiotic and interdependent in nature. In organizations, this phase is characterized by:

- Individuation changes to a sense of 'we',
- Staff drive the organization with a sense of purpose,
- The value base is strengthened,
- The organization is inclusive and effective; and

- Recognition comes through performance or results one is producing.

Organizations naturally evolve through these three phases although they may not be as distinct as outlined above. The characteristics described in the table entitled Team and Organizational assessment below can help pinpoint the dominant phase. Once the organization has shifted, there is no going back without starting over again. The birth of the new is often accompanied by a crisis. Crisis is an important catalyst for the shift to take place and the organization to break through to a new level of potential. However, a crisis that is not well handled can kill an organization. The key issue is that an organization may choose to anticipate change and prepare for it or have it forced upon it.

Many challenges organizations face can be better understood through its stage of development. This will also affect the type of interventions that will be most effective. The challenge is to recognize the organization's present stage and prepare it to consciously move toward the next. Most organizational improvement efforts are ultimately aimed at creating an interdependent phase organization.

A summary of the above model is given in appendix 2. The second model is the 'levels of complexity' model. This model is presented below:

Levels of Complexity Model

A bee sting can only be cured by uprooting the sting
If the shadow of the tree is crooked, straighten the tree not the shadow

An organization called us to help them as they were experiencing high levels of staff turnover. Management thought people were leaving because of poor conditions of service. We suggested that before addressing the problem we needed to conduct an assessment so that we could get the facts right. The assessment revealed that the organization did not have any problem with its conditions of service.

In fact, its conditions of service were among the best. The real problem of the organization was poor relationships. There were factions led by different department heads. The factions were fighting fiercely and psychologically wearing each other out. This made frustrated many members of staff opt out. Some left for less paying jobs or for no new jobs at all just for 'peace of mind'. This story illustrates the importance of understanding the level of complexity at which an organizational challenge or even opportunity is occurring.

The 'levels of complexity model' is a framework used in understanding organizations. It shows different 'levels' that constitut es an organization and their interrelationships that comprise an organization. It also shows that as one moves from the 'outer' or 'surface' to the 'inner' and 'deeper' levels, it becomes more and more complicated to address the organizational problems or recognize the opportunities. In addition to being a model for understanding organizations, the framework is also a diagnostic tool to assess the 'health statuses of an organization. It can also guide appropriate interventions on the issues identified in the assessment.

In assessing the 'health status' of the organization and facilitating interventions to address identified issues, it becomes more and more complicated to both identify and intervene when moving from the outer and more tangible elements, like resources and skills, to more intangible elements, like values and culture.

The model is called *levels of complexity* because it shows the different elements of an organization and as well as the increasing complexity when moving between the tangible to the intangible. In practice, the model is used to: identify strengths the organization can build upon; identify threats the organization needs to address; surface deeper issues hindering the organization; and help people take a holistic approach in addressing organizational issues.

The model begins with the most basic concern of immediate sustainability. In order to survive, grow and excel, an organization must have adequate financial and material resources. Its people must also have adequate and relevant skills and competencies to attract the needed material and financial resources.

An organization's policies, procedures and systems affect its decision-making, accountability and communication. They are also where the perception of fairness is derived. A sense of fairness strengthens relationships among peers and between subordinates and supervisors, engendering a team spirit and conducive organizational culture. The next level concerning the structure of roles and responsibilities and how they are shared also strengthens relationships if they are clear and well defined.

Strategy represents its best options to guide an organization's use of resources (both human and financial) to pursue its mission. The strategic plan enables the organization to build on its strengths, take advantage of opportunities and address threats in the task environment. Strategic planning enables the organization to consciously respond to the changes taking place both inside and outside of the organization and influence these changes as much as possible. The aim of strategic planning is to prepare today's organization for the future because failing to plan is planning to fail.

The vision, mission and values constitute an organization's spirit. The vision is what in society the organization would like to see changed as a result of its work. The shared idea of creating an ideal society is the driving force behind healthy organizations and a significant factor in individual and team commitment and motivation. The mission is the organization's specific contribution to their societal vision. Usually, the vision is too big for one organization to achieve single-handedly while the mission is concerned with the specific questions of identity: who are we? Why do we exist? Who do we serve and where are they?

Organizational culture is based on the values and behaviours that people consider important and are consciously or unconsciously rewarded whenever practiced. There are two types of values: business values (that the organization must practice when dealing with its customers) and people values (that the people must practice internally to create a favorable working environment).

Lastly, the task environment is the context in which the organization operates, offering it challenges, threats and opportunities. All the levels are interconnected, improving these elements holistically builds the organization's capacity to address challenges and threats and make use of its opportunities, thereby having an impact in society in the direction of its ideal.

The Levels of Complexity Model

Level of Complexity	Explanation
1. Financial and material resources	Money, offices, equipment, computers, photocopiers, etc. of the organization
2. Skills and competencies	People's type, level, relevance and quality of the knowledge and skills in the organization
3. Policies, procedures and systems	The rules and regulations aimed at facilitating work and ensuring fairness and legality
4. Structure	The hierarchy and how roles and responsibilities are shared among the people in the organization
5. Strategy	How the organization has planned to use its resources in achieving its mission and goals
6. Vision and mission	What the organization wants to see changed in the environment as a result of its work; the reason for its existence
7. Organizational culture	The 'way we do our things in this organization'; the accepted norms, values and behaviours in organization
8. Task environment	The political, economic, socio-cultural and technological factors impacting the organization

Source: Olive Subscription Service (1997: 30)

The 'levels of complexity model' has been chosen to frame this book on proverbs for four reasons:

1. It is an analytical tool that shows that in any organizational system, a problem may arise from one or more sources or levels.
2. It is a guide to the type of interventions undertaken to address a problem based on the level of its cause. For example, the lack of adequate funds is addressed by raising and diversifying funding sources while relationship problems are addressed through team building.
3. It is an indicator of the amount of effort and energy an organization needs to address the problem. The higher the level in the model, the more complex the intervention. Lack of funding can be solved with a donor's check, but the lack of shared values among staff cannot be solved overnight.
4. It shows where the organization should holistically focus its efforts. Addressing lower level needs like training staff while ignoring higher level needs like a shared vision and mission will not improve organizational effectiveness in the long run. The model demonstrates what an effective organization is like and how it can be built.

There are three main approaches for building an "ideal" organization and they are: (1) acquiring more money and resources; (2) Training current staff and board members; and (3) Facilitating process interventions. Many organizations believe that with more money they could build stronger organizations. Others try to build ideal organizations through training. These lower factors (money, material resources and training opportunities) are the easiest to address since they are often more tangible as compared to higher factors (policies, systems and procedures; relationships, values and culture; vision and mission; and environmental factors). This explains why injecting resources and training to address felt needs have been the traditional means of building organizational capacity in the past.

Efforts of growth (funding and training) that preoccupy most organizations fail to address the problem of ineffectiveness. For this problem to be adequately addressed, organizational growth must be combined with process interventions. Process interventions concentrate on the higher levels of complexity. Since these are usually unfelt in most organizations, process interventions awaken consciousness and bring about an appropriate foundation upon which to base funding and training interventions.

Process interventions, therefore, form the bedrock for the creation of the ideal organization described above and also form a foundation for sustainable funding and training.

1. Clarifying Objectives and Scope

In addition to raising awareness, the purpose of the assessment must be clarified at the beginning of the process. Most organizations use self-assessment as an organizational improvement tool. Assessments can be done with top management in strategic planning work or even at the lowest levels of the organization with the aim of identifying opportunities for improvement. The scope must specify whether the assessment will cover the whole organization or just some parts of it like departments or divisions.

An understanding of the phases of organization development and levels of complexity models provides a comprehensive understanding of how an effective organization would look and behave. According to (Kaplan 1999: 14, 15) an effective organization:

- Has a clear and shared vision that consciously guides its activities;
- Has clear and shared values that guide behaviour through daily practice, not simply superficially conversation;
- Has strong and inspiring leadership that facilitates and does not hinder work;
- Has effective strategies and demand driven activities. It is not paralyzed by the vastness of problems in the environment or within itself. It directs its energy toward what it can do, rather

than mourning over what it cannot do;
▪ Takes time to consciously learn from its practice and uses internal and external learning as its basis for improvement;
▪ Takes time to develop its staff beyond academic qualifications to maximize their potential contribution and emphasize self-mastery;
▪ Collaborates effectively with its stakeholders;
▪ Has adequate, self-sustaining financial and material resources.

This stage also involves creating a word picture or a picture of the desired situation. An example is given below of the word picture of the Human Rights Centre (HRC) (A fictitious name of a civil society organization):

Human Rights Center's (HRC) desired situation

The year is 20xx (5 years from now). HRC is financially independent. It has its offices in its own building. It has sufficient competent and skilled staff and volunteers in all its areas of work.

HRC has effective policies, systems and procedures in the areas of:
- Human resource
- Administration
- Finances
- Monitoring and Evaluation
  Conditions of Service

HRC has a clear structure that is understood by all and the structure is adhered to. The structure is clearly linked to a clear strategy and an empowering shared vision and mission.

The members of staff are conscious of the culture and values of the organization and are consciously working at creating and maintaining a healthy organizational climate.

> HRC is consciously building its internal capacity and identifying strategic organizations and institutions for partnership and collaboration.
>
> HRC is implementing effective programmes and activities that are focused enough to make impact. The activities are based on objective research and documentation and they are being systematically monitored and evaluated

Such a picture provides a benchmark towards what the organization must work. The key questions in the actual assessment are, "what can help us to realize the ideal picture" and "what can prevent us from realizing the ideal picture?"

2. Selecting the Proverbs Organizational Self-assessment Tools or Other Methods

There are many frameworks for self-assessment. The African Proverbs self-assessment tool is presented in appendix 1. Among the other strengths of the African proverbs self-assessment tool are its strength and ability to add humour to the otherwise very sensitive organizational issues. The proverbs also are catalysts for generating dialogue among the people involved in the assessment. The rating enables the group to reach objective conclusions through consensus.

3. Form the Assessment Team

Teams better do organizational assessments because individuals may not have adequate in-depth knowledge of the organization and the tool being used. Different people may see the same things differently. Taking different views enhances objectivity.

4. **Plan the Assessment**

   This stage looks at the issues of how the data and information will actually be collected and who will be the actual people collecting the data and information. The analysis of the data will also be planned at this stage. A time schedule will be vital to guide this process.

5. **Collect the Relevant Data**

   Self-assessment must be as objective as possible. It must be based on fact and not opinion. The proverb organization assessment tool works best in focus group discussion settings. To add objectivity, however, it may be necessary to triangulate the findings with other methods of collecting data using different tools like questionnaires, individual interviews, document analysis, observation etc.

6. **Analyzing the Data in a Feedback Workshop**

   When you are pointing a finger of blame at another person remember that the remaining four are pointing back at you

   This involves presenting the 'raw findings' in a feedback workshop for participatory analysis. The people are given the findings to analyze. This involves distilling issues from the findings and clarifying where the findings were not clear. It involves separating facts from perceptions. It works better when the feedback workshop is done at some quiet place away from the office to avoid interruptions and enhance concentration. A key point is helping the client to own the successes and challenges of the organization and, most importantly, to help the client not to externalize the challenges or problems.

7. Action Planning

After the participatory analysis the next stage is to prioritize the identified issues and to agree on the interventions that will be required to address them. The people then agree on the interventions as shown in the table above. The team will also agree on who will be responsible, when the intervention will happen and what the indicators for achievement will be. The action plan can be used as a basis for measuring progress.

There are 13 Major OD 'family' Interventions as Shown Below:

ACTIVITY	PURPOSE
1. Diagnostic	to ascertain problems, traditional data-collection and fact-finding methods are commonly used, including interviews and questionnaires
2. Team building	to enhance the effective operation of systems
3. Inter-group	to improve effectiveness of independent groups. The focus is on joint activities
4. Survey feedback	Analyzing data produced by a survey and designing appropriate action plans based on collected data
5. Education and training	to improve skills, abilities and knowledge of individuals
6. Restructuring	to improve the effectiveness of the technical or structural aspects affecting individuals or groups. Examples include job enrichment, matrix structures and MBO
7. Process consultation	to help managers understand and act on human processes in the organizations such as leadership, co-operation and conflict (led by the consultant)
8. Grid organisation development	a six-phase change model involving the entire organization (developed by Blake and Mouton)
9. Third party peace making	to manage conflict between two parties, and conducted by a third party, usually a skilled

	consultant
10. Coaching and counselling	to better enable individuals to define learning goals, reflect on how others see their behaviour, explore alternative behaviours and learn new ones
11. Life and career planning	to help individuals identify life and career objectives, capabilities, areas of strengths and deficiency, and strategies for achieving objectives
12. Planning and goal setting	To include theory and experience in planning and goal setting. May be conducted at individual, group or organizational levels
13. Strategic management	to help key policy makers identify their organization's basic mission and goals; ascertain environmental demands, threats, and opportunities; and engage in long range action planning

Source: French & Bell 1995

Factors Hindering Effective Use of Organizational Assessments

There are a number of factors hindering the effective use of organizational assessments. A few are described below:

- *Lack of ownership*: One of the major observations we have made is that many organizations lack ownership of the organizational assessment process. Not many see value in an assessment and very few actually call to have one done. Many organizations undertake assessments at a donor's request as a means towards getting money. The assessments are done for the donor. Once they get the money, the motivation to implement the capacity building plan wanes.
- *No Culture of Prevention:* In most developing countries, there is not a strong tradition of having personal health checkups done regularly. People wait until they are really sick before seeking medical attention. The same thinking applies to the way organizations are run. As long as the pain is not felt, there is no reason for an assessment. It is conducted when the

problem is serious, even though it could have been prevented earlier.

- *Fear of Weaknesses:* Many organizations are not willing to disclose their weaknesses. They look at assessments as a way of 'exposing' the organization. Such an attitude makes people reluctant and not authentic during the actual assessment process.
- *Lack of Donor Support:* The end product of an organizational assessment is a capacity building plan. Building the capacity of an organization is a long-term process and requires a long-term commitment. However, many donors are not enthusiastic about supporting organizations in this way and for that long. The paradox is that many donors are concerned with improving organizational performance without thinking about what produces that performance. Capacity building requires money. Without financial support the plan may not be fully implemented and the health of the organization may not be fully improved.
- *Inattention to Process:* Lack of a process-orientation among organizational change agents is another major hindrance to the effective use of organizational assessments. Many consultants still believe that all organizational problems can be solved by acquiring money and providing training. To the man with only a hammer in his toolkit, all problems look like nails. Similarly, consultants often try to fix all problems with training. Most deep rooted problems organizations face cannot be resolved by training but need long-term process interventions. Trainings may not go deep enough but only produce superficial and short-lived results.
- *Not Investing Adequate Time:* Organizations working in very challenging environments are often overwhelmed by the magnitude of the need they see. As a result, they end up getting caught up in a culture of 'busyness' that takes up all their time, leaving none for internal reflection and learning. In

this case, no time is left for using the organizational assessments or implementing the capacity building plan.

- *No Monitoring Systems:* Many organizations lack effective monitoring and evaluation systems at both secretariat and board levels. The problem is more serious at the board level. Without effective monitoring and evaluation systems, organizations are not able to objectively assess their progress. This is complicated by the fact that most monitoring and evaluation systems are only concerned with the organization's performance and not its 'internal health'. The assessment is forgotten and not valued.
- *Poor Leadership:* All the above factors are tied to the problem of absent visionary and effective leadership. Leaders who cannot see that the long-term performance and success of an organization is tied to its internal health will not value organizational assessments and their implementation.

I was fortunate to meet a former vice president of my country at Jomo Kenyatta International Airport in Nairobi and spent some time with him while we were waiting for a flight. I asked him what he was doing after leaving office. He told me, he was devoting much of his time and energy in helping efforts aimed at fighting the HIV and AIDS pandemic. He shared with me some of his reflections on the challenges such efforts are facing. He said if the efforts are to be effective, it is important to think through some parameters like: what is the message we must bring to the people and which groups of people? Who should bring the message? How should they bring it? When and where should they bring it? He told me of a woman cancer breast expert he knew who tried to sensitize women on the importance of regularly going for breast cancer testing. The people in the area were very religious and she felt the best place to meet the women was at churches after church services. To her surprise, very few and in some cases no woman at all remained after the church services. Later, investigations showed her that women could not stay back because soon after church service, they had to rush home to cook for the family (and Sunday was the only day the whole family could be together) and many times also entertain visitors. This was a very important value for the women in comparison to hearing a lecture on breast cancer. The lady changed her approach by thinking through the appropriate message, messenger, how the message should be packaged, when and where. She discovered that the best place to find the women was at hair saloons. At the hair saloons, they could spend hours upon hours in a relaxed and non-rushing atmosphere. In addition, most of the women went to hair dressers who were personal friends. This provided a more conducive and receptive environment. The lady then targeted the hair saloon workers and trained them to talk with the women about the importance of breast cancer testing. Needless to say, the rates of breast cancer testing shot through the roof.

If organizational assessments and OD interventions in general are to be more effective, it is also important to think through the same parameters. The message must be positive. People in the organization must see the purpose as being to build the organization for their organizational and personal benefit rather than fault finding. The messenger or the leaders and consultants and even donors must be people of integrity. If people don't trust the leaders, they will not trust the purpose and the process. A very skilled and experienced health worker was talking with a group of village women on the importance of family planning and; small and manageable families. Everything was going on well until towards the end when one of the women asked her how many children she had. She reluctantly said she had seven. That watered down her entire message, no matter how much she tried to explain why she had seven children. Her integrity was put to question.

It is also important to think about when OD interventions would be more effective. Assessments and OD interventions in general are more effective when they address a felt need, aspiration or a specific pain in the organization. It is sometimes important to wait for the organization to experience pain first or in the case of preventive interventions a lot of consciousness awakening must be done to enable people to see that the current good situation is not the best and that they can be and do better for the benefit of the organization and themselves.

How the assessment or the interventions are done is also important. Each organization and context is unique. Some situations will require dealing with whole organizations; others will require dealing with only parts of the organization or just individuals. In one assessment exercise, most members of staff and the board kept telling us that the problems of the organization would be solved if the director (who actually had called us) was fired.

Finally, assessments are more effective when the feedback workshop or session is carried out at a place away from the familiar environment of the organization. This creates psychological time and space for more objective and clear thinking among the participants.

Conclusion

The chapter has discussed the organizational assessment process. It has also presented two organizational assessment models, *the stages of development* and the *levels of complexity* models. The output of an organizational assessment is an organizational capacity building plan. The plan outlines the interventions that the organizations will need in order to build its internal, implementation and collaboration or networking capacity. The plan also identifies the people in the organization responsible for the implementation of the plan, the indicators of success and the sequencing of the interventions. Just as *when the lion is running and stops to look back, it is not that the lion is afraid but is rather trying to see the distance he has covered*, it is important once in a while for every organization or even individuals to take a break and see the distance they have covered. This is not a sign of fear but rather strength. To be effective, organizational assessments must surface root causes of issues rather than just dealing with symptoms – *do not look where you have fallen but rather look at where you have tripped*.

The next chapters will discuss some OD interventions beginning from individual to team through organization wide interventions.

Conducting Organizational Assessments

How do the following proverbs help us to understand the importance of organizational assessments?

One cannot arrive at their destination in life if they do not understand how they arrived at where they are today

When the lion is running and stops to look back, it is not that the lion is afraid but rather he is trying to see the distance he has s Covered.

Health is wealth

How does the following proverb help us to own the challenges our organization is facing?

When you are pointing a finger of blame at another person, remember that the remaining four are pointing back at you

How does the following proverb help us to understand at what stage of development our organization is and how this is helping us to understand the type of challenges the organization is meeting?

Even the biggest rooster that crows the loudest was once upon a time just an egg

It is better to be the head of a mouse than the tail of a lion

How does the following proverb help us identify the appropriate levels at which our organization should address its challenges?

A bee sting can only be cured by uprooting the sting

If the shadow of the tree is crooked, straighten the tree not the shadow

What does the following proverb teach us about dealing with problems at their source/cause?

If you can't stop the monkeys from coming to the banana tree, cut down the banana tree

CHAPTER THREE

Self-Development

The greatest investment one can make is to invest in oneself
A stream cannot rise above its source
The poorest person is not one without money but the one without a vision

Introduction

All living systems grow and develop from within. They do not grow and develop from outside. All living systems have within themselves the 'program and ingredients' not only to grow and develop but also to thrive in any environment they find themselves in. A baobab tree has within its seed the 'program and ingredients' to multiply itself into a baobab forest. No baobab tree can develop another baobab tree. No any other tree can develop another tree. Similarly, no human being can develop another human being. Other people may help or hinder but they cannot develop one. Every human being has within himself or herself the 'program and ingredients' for development. The key difference between those who make use of this fact and those that do not is 'consciousnesses and its application.

My personal experience of self-development coincided with my introduction to the field of organization development as a trainee OD consultant. It has since formed the foundation and the essence of all my practice. The greatest insight I got is that *you cannot 'develop' others if you are not developed yourself.* This is why holistically the leader must be a few steps ahead of the followers.

A stream cannot rise above its source. Similarly, organizations are only as good as the people working inside them. No organization can rise above the collective level of the people it employs. Improving the effectiveness of the organization therefore has to do with improving the effectiveness of the individuals working in the organization. The greatest investment that people in the organization can make is for each one of them to take responsibility for investing in themselves. This fact is becoming increasingly recognized and a number of organizations are adopting various forms of staff development activities. There is a strong observation, however, that in most cases, staff development is equated to staff training. It is supposed that if members of staff will acquire sufficient knowledge, skills and competencies, they will become more effective. Despite the observation that a purely 'training' approach has left more to be desired, most organizations have not discovered its alternatives or complements.

Knowledge, skills and competencies are not enough for personal effectiveness. We all have seen ineffective organizations made up of highly qualified people and we have also seen highly effective organizations made up of not so highly qualified people. Self-development is the missing link. Self -development is the foundation upon which if the knowledge, skills and competencies are built, they become truly useful to the individual and the organization.

Unfortunately, literature on Self-development in organizations, especially that which is applicable to the developing regions and development organizations is scanty. Many organizational leaders do not know what Self-development is, how to go about it and what its benefits to the organization might be. The need for organizational effectiveness cannot be overemphasized and as such Self-development of the individuals working within the organizations must get even greater attention. Organizational people exist to serve other people as stipulated in the mission statements of their organizations. They are change agents. But one cannot facilitate the change process in others unless they have undergone their own change processes first. One cannot give what they do not have. This is the major explanation of the failure of many development efforts and the essence of Self-development. The more an individual develops him or herself, the more he or she will be able to help others in their own processes of Self-development. It is now being increasingly

| Chapter Three | Chiku Malunga
Organizational Wisdom in 100 African Proverbs (An Introduction to Organizational Paremiology)
London & Abuja, Adonis & Abbey Publishers |

recognized that the only effective development intervention is self-development.

This chapter, therefore, addresses four main areas. These are: the meaning of self-development, the importance of self-development, the process of self-development and challenges to overcome.

The Meaning of Self-development

A self-controlled person is stronger that the person who can conquer many cities
A changed place cannot transform a person but a transformed person can change a place

Self-Development is a process that ensures personal and organizational effectiveness by enabling individuals create a vision and mission for one's life, recognizing and paying adequate attention to the roles one plays in life, identifying goals in each of the roles, organizing one's time, consciously practicing empowering values and implementing activities with the aim of achieving the goals on a day to day basis and consciously getting feedback on how one is doing. Self-development helps an individual to focus and continually refocus on what contribution he or she can make to the organization he or she is working in.

Self-development is a personal journey of self-discovery. Through self-development one discovers his or her hidden potentials and learns how to utilize them effectively for his or her own benefit and the people he or she serves. Self-development is a continuous process of bringing one's shadow to light. The shadow is that part of ours that we are not aware of and therefore hinders our effectiveness. The shadow represents the unconsciousness of our contradictions which stand in the way of realizing our developmental desires. By bringing the shadow to light we release our potential.

At birth, each individual is born with potential, which is supposed to be translated into actual achievement throughout life until one's death. Self-development is the process of translating this potential into achievements. The more one becomes aware and skilled in recognizing and tapping into this potential, the more he or she will live a life of achievement and satisfaction and die 'empty' with all his or her potential utilized. In other words, such an individual will live a full life- may be not necessarily in terms of length but depth. Self-development therefore is a process of continually and consciously focusing and refocusing on what one truly wants in life through continuous reflection and action.

People practicing self-development, therefore, approach life creatively as an assignment with a definite beginning and definite end, a time period in which they have to release all the potential that is within them. They take self-development to be the process of knowing and working on oneself, achieved through conscious and continuous questioning of everything, not taking anything for granted, looking beneath and behind the skills and techniques one is taught, at the underlying paradigms so that one obtains mastery over them, freedom to challenge and adapt and refashion.

People practicing self-development approach life as an assignment, which begins at birth and ends on the day one dies. The purpose of their life is to make a contribution towards making the world a better place for themselves, others and future generations to live in. They look at life as a mission.

Self-development enables the individual to respond to different situations differently and appropriately rather than responding to all the situations the same way. Facilitating processes of change in systems and other people's lives calls for responses from different parts of oneself; and different approaches and modalities at different times. Unfortunately in most of us many parts of ourselves especially in the subconscious have not been used; are hidden from ourselves and are thus untapped.

In the organization, self-development may mean different things to different people because individuals at different stages of development in their lives look at life differently. The role of the organization, therefore, is not to define in concrete terms what self-development is or should be but to create an environment in which each individual will be free to follow their own paths of self-development and then to harness the individual benefits for total organizational effectiveness. Self-development is the development of the flexibility of the self to effectively respond to the environment and its changing demands. Inability to respond to the environment and its changing demands leads to personal ineffectiveness. It leads to the creation of mental walls of self-imposed limitations. The discipline of self-development challenges one to make challenging demands upon oneself. It is a general observation that if an individual demands little of himself or herself, they will never rise above mediocrity.

Self-Development Assessment Tool

Rate yourself and explain why you give yourself that rate.
Rate 0- 5   0 = Non – existent   5 = Excellent

1. How conscious am I about the importance of self-development?
   - The person who doesn't know where she is going will not get there.
   - If a child washes his hands he will eat with kings.
   - The greatest achievement is to master oneself.
2. How clear is the vision and purposes of my life?
   - The eyes that have seen the sea cannot be satisfied by a mere lagoon.
   - What the eyes have seen the heart cannot forget.
3. How conscious am I about the importance of self-leadership?
   - It is better to be the head of a mouse than a tail of a lion.
4. How conscious am I about who I am and my potential?
   - An eagle that does not know that it is an eagle, lives like a chicken
   - It is better to fail with originality than succeed with imitation
5. How conscious am I about what values and behaviours that I must embrace to ensure the realization of my vision– accomplishment of my vision and mission?
   - The river that forgets its sources will soon dry up
   - If money grew on trees many people would be married to monkeys.
6. How conscious am I about the contradictions in my values or behaviours that would prevent me from realizing my vision and accomplishing my mission?

-Many people smear themselves with mud and then complain that they are dirty.

-When you are pointing a finger of blame at someone the remaining four are pointing back at yourself-Judge each day not by its harvest but by the seeds you sow in to it.

7. How conscious am I about the need to concentrate and focus my energy on a few key priority areas for impact and realization of my vision and mission?

    -The dog that belongs to everyone in the village will die of starvation.

    -A hunter with one arrow does not shoot at careless aim

    -Rays of light concentrated through a lens can set an entire forest ablaze.

8. How independent am I in my decision making and actions?

    -If two wise men agree on everything, then there is no need for one of them.

    -If you want your voice to be heard simply talk.

9. How conscious am I about the need for a mentor in my life and how well am I working with the mentor?

    -What old people see while seated, young people may not see standing on their toes.

10. How well do I handle negative feedback from my mentor and other people in my life?

    - Because of lack of criticism, the warthog's teeth have grown disproportionately long

11. How careful am I about the choice of my mentor or source of advice?

    -Advice is like mushrooms. The wrong kind can be fatal.

12. How well am I sequencing my steps with my journey towards self-development?

    -No matter how hungry you are, you can only eat your food one mouthful at a time

13. How conscious am I about the need for patience in the journey towards self

    -mastery?

    -Take it easy with the drum the night is still long.

    -Shortcuts are full of mud.

> -A patient mouse in a young banana plant will one day eat a ripe banana.
> -The journey of a thousand miles starts with one step.
>
> 14. How conscious am I about my limitations and the need to work with them rather than against them?
>   -The dry grass should not challenge the fire.
>   -It was ignorance that made the rat to challenge the cat to a wrestling match.
>   -It is a stupid dog that barks at an elephant.
>   - An egg has no business dancing with the stones
> 15. How well do I manage obstacles, challenges and setbacks in my journey of self-development?
>   -A person is taller than any mountain they have climbed.
> 16. How well and fast do I carry out my intentions and resolutions?
>   -Good intentions are like babies crying in church they should be carried out immediately.
>   -Ideas are like a baby, easy to conceive but difficult to deliver
>   -Don't tell people what you will do; show them what you have done.

Self-Development and Organization Development

The organization is an extension of the individual. Organization development is an extension of self-development. Effective organization development must be linked to and be based on effective self-development.

Like individuals, organizations are tripartite. They exist at three levels of the body, mind and spirit.

The body of the organization is its material and financial resources. The mind is comprised of: skills and competences, the structure and how the work is shared, the relationships in the organization, the policies, systems and procedures; and the strategy the organization is pursuing. The spirit of the organization comprises the core issues of vision and purpose and identity (mission, culture, values, attitudes and beliefs).

The foundation of organizational effectiveness or performance is in its spiritual dimensions. Just like individuals however or because organizations are made up of people they tend to focus more on the body and partly the mind. The spirit is mostly unconscious.

If individuals are trying to help others, and their own lives suffer from the same malady, they will not be able to effectively help others and organizations to move to higher levels of performance. *If a person offers to give you a cloth, first check what they are wearing themselves.* Development has been defined as the awakening of consciousness. Self-development can therefore be defined as the awakening of those aspects of our individual and organizational lives that we are not conscious of and then using this awakening in improving personal and organizational effectiveness.

As explained elsewhere, there are three complementary ways for improving organizational effectiveness. These are: provision of financial and material resources, provision of skills and competencies and facilitation of process interventions. The organizational body is developed through the acquisition of financial and material resources. The organizational mind is developed through the provision of skills and competencies. The organizational spirit is developed through process interventions.

To be truly effective, individuals must develop their capacities through: acquisition of financial and material resources; continuous training and retraining to continually develop and update one's skills and competencies and; undergoing spiritual and mental process interventions that will awaken the consciousness for intuition, conscience and communion.

The Purpose of Self-Development

One cannot know another person without first knowing oneself
There are no short cuts to the top of a palm tree
If a child washes his hands he will eat with kings
The able blacksmith will never lack work

Who we are determines what we can do and how we can do it. In other words our 'being' precedes our 'doing'. Most efforts to improve personal effectiveness however have focused on and emphasized the 'doing' part. People have been trained in so many skills or how to do this or that thing better but not much corresponding effort has been made on helping people to improve their 'being' which determines their doing.

While the 'doing' can be developed through training, the 'being' lies beneath where most conventional training can reach. And as long as the 'doing' and 'being' are not in sync, much of the training directed at the 'doing' does not yield maximum benefits. The challenge of personal effectiveness therefore is to bring the 'being and the 'doing' to the same level. Self-development makes this possible by primarily targeting the 'being' and making it the rightful foundation upon which the 'doing' is based. Reflecting on the life of Victor Frankl, Haddon quoted in Covey (2004: 315) summarizes the essence of the purpose of self-development when he observes that,

"For Frankl, since spirituality is in its essence self-transcendence, it brings with it human freedom. But it is not *from* as much as freedom *to*. We are not free from our biological nature, whether instinctual drives, genetic legacies, or the functions or malfunctions of our brains and bodies. Nor are we free from the grasp of social, developmental, and environmental influences. But we are free to take a stand towards these, even against them. We are free to do what we will with the cards we are dealt with, to choose what response we will make to fateful events, to decide what cause or person will receive our devotion.

And this *freedom to* carry an *obligation to*. Each of us is responsible for something, to someone. By using our freedom to act responsibly in the world, we uncover meaning in our lives. It is only when our will to meaning is frustrated that we settle for the pursuit of personal pleasure (Freud), or financial and social success (Adler).

When a person exercises spiritual freedom and responsibility, there follows a host of effects: peace of mind, good conscience, and contentment. But these occur naturally– as by-products, so to speak.

But pursuing any of these directly makes their attainment improbable or impossible. There is nothing quite like striving for peace of mind to keep one edgy. To center ones effort on achieving a good conscience may lead to hypocrisy or guilt– or both. To make health one's chief aim may bring on something akin to hypochondria. For Frankl, these are not the ends to be pursued for their own sake for one's own good. Instead, they ensue naturally for persons who live for something else, for something greater".

Organizational Benefits of Self-Development

The primary justification for self-development is that most organizations are operating below their potential, the main reason being that people leading them and consultants helping them are also operating below potential. Since these are the people primarily responsible for change in the organizations, they cannot give what they do not have themselves. When organizational leaders start practicing the discipline of self-development, they raise their own and therefore the performance of the organization. When they start appreciating the pre-eminence of issues like personal vision and purpose, they naturally affect their organizational visions, purposes, goals and directions. Self-development being contagious, their influence on others to seek their own paths of self -development goes in ripples.

For organizational development to take place, personal change must precede organizational change. In organizational capacity building efforts, we have observed that attention has mostly been given to organization's wide interventions with little if any on self-development. The main reason could be that the people bringing about the change process (the leaders and consultants) have not themselves undergone self-development processes in their own lives. The more they develop themselves, the more they are also able to help the people they work with and therefore entire organizations.

Self-development is the means of bringing to consciousness those aspects of organizational life that have the most impact on organizational life. A central feature of self-development is the ability

Chapter Three	Chiku Malunga
	Organizational Wisdom in 100 African Proverbs (An Introduction to Organizational Paremiology)
	London & Abuja, Adonis & Abbey Publishers

to face the truth without fear. *It is understandable when children fear the darkness but the real tragedy of life is when grownups fear and hide from the light.* The individual going through the self-development process does not fear but cherishes feedback. When the organization is made up of people who are practicing the discipline of self-development, they are able to give each other feedback and therefore bring to light the hidden aspects of the organization. It is only when these parts have been brought to light that the organization can move from its stuck points.

Self-development ensures organizational learning. Organizational learning cannot happen when the individuals within it are not learning. Efforts to create a learning organization can only be appreciated and sustained by individuals who are themselves learning. Self-development brings together the needs of the organization and the individual. This ensures a 'psychological contract' or a deeper connection between the individual and the organization.

An organization with individuals pursuing their own paths of self-development is likely to attract and retain staff than the one that is not because people pursuing self-development take organizational change and challenges that would otherwise frustrate other employees as their own responsibility. Self-development develops an individual's resilience, which helps him or her to avoid seeking the route of least resistance as a means of avoiding pain. A person going through self-development embraces pain as being a very important ally of his or her own development process. They recognize that pain; the pain of contradiction between the real and the ideal is a major motivation for the development process itself. This ability to embrace pain enables the person to stay on in the organization and work towards making it a more effective organization rather than 'escaping to greener pastures'. The person going through a self-development process recognizes that a *wise man marries the woman he loves; a wiser man loves the woman he marries.*

Self-development enables the individual to respond differently and appropriately to different situations and times. Self-development makes possible the practice of professionalism, which is in addition to the observance of rigor, means the ability to provide unique responses to unique situations. *When the beat of the drum changes so must the step of the dance.* Lastly, self- development enables one to live a full life – one is able to balance work, family and social life through enhanced consciousness of the roles one plays in life and how to go about them.

Personal Benefits of Self- Development

Self-development enables one to have clarity of one's purpose in life– the individual knows who she or he is and his or her mission in life. The sense of purpose and direction will permeate the entire being and he or she will be able to anticipate what happens next – be proactive rather than be on the receiving end of life. Recognizing one's identity and purpose enables the individual to be what he or she was meant to be.

Self-development enables one to practice openness in communication, he or she is non-defensive, willing and able to express thoughts and feelings simply and directly, ask for what he or she wants from others while leaving them free to say yes or no. He or she is also able to say yes or no without feeling guilty. Since such a person's chief aim in life is clear, they are clear on what to say yes to and what to say no to without feeling guilty. They say yes to what will aid them towards their life chief aim and they say no to what will hinder them in their journey towards their life chief aim.

Self-development enables one to listen effectively and enables individuals to actively seek feedback on how his or her behaviour affects them and others. He or she is free with both positive and negative feedback. The individual uses the feedback to learn and change his or her behaviour for more effectiveness.

Self-development gives the ability for self-expression and the capacity to be – the capacity for enjoying, getting pleasure and being involved in the now – in the present, the individual is not stuck in the past or the future. In addition, self-development contributes to personal happiness. Self-development gives the individual the flexibility to try new and more effective ways of doing things and relating to others. It enables an individual to choose from a wide range of behaviours – to choose the most appropriate behaviour for the situation at hand. It also enables an individual to empathize with others – to see and accept others as they are – to appreciate the uniqueness and singularity of others.

In short Self-Development ensures personal effectiveness and satisfaction. It also enables the creation and development of personal and business relationships.

The Self-Development Process

Life is like riding a bicycle; you don't fall off unless you stop pedaling
A person is taller than every mountain he or she has climbed

Self-development is a process; it is a journey and a solitary one. The key words in self-development are Quietitude, Solitude, Reflection, Consciousness, Feedback and Meditation.

It is important to point out that for self-development to thrive in an organization, the policies, systems and procedures of the organization especially in the areas of personnel planning, career planning, performance appraisal, salary reviews etc must support and reward self-development. In other words, the organization must create a conducive environment for self-development to thrive. The organization must create space and time for self-development.

For individuals, it is important to keep a self-development journal and take regular and periodic breaks into solitude and quietitude for reflection. A self-development journal is a great aid in one's personal journey of self-development. In it one writes his or her goals, achievements and failures. In it one also notes his or her observations of patterns and trends in his or her life. A self-development journal plays a key role in enhancing one's 'reflective' capabilities. A self-development journal helps one get lessons and insights from the art of living.

Chapter Three	Chiku Malunga
	Organizational Wisdom in 100 African Proverbs (An Introduction to Organizational Paremiology)
	London & Abuja, Adonis & Abbey Publishers

There are four main stages to the self-development process. These are: the Realization for the need of self-development, the self-assessment, action planning and adopting and routinizing interventions.

The Realization Stage

This is the shaking of the status quo arising from one or more of the following:

A realization that a once useful behaviour in a major area of life has stopped being helpful or has actually become counterproductive. An example would be the realization that a 'controlling' approach has lost its effect on a teenage son or daughter.

A realization that one's personal needs have significantly changed and current efforts are no longer helping me fulfill my needs. An example would be a job that used to give one tremendous joy and challenge which has now stopped to give the individual meaning.

A realization that the pace of change in the environment is far out pacing my capacity to cope. The realization that tomorrow I may be faced with responsibilities and challenges that I have not fully prepared for. An example may be the need for financial independence. The realization makes the individual see and appreciates the need for personal change and it may also give insight into the type of change one may need to pursue.

Self-Assessment Stage

This stage involves getting the opportunity to reflect on the desired situation and the current reality and establish the gaps in a non-threatening environment. It also involves reflecting on the 'consequences I am getting from my actions'. This stage is mainly involved with getting feedback in various forms both from oneself and from others. The African proverbs based self-assessment tool above gives a useful tool for this stage.

Action Plan

This stage is concerned with developing action points on how the gap between the real and the ideal will be bridged. It will also involve setting indicators, targets and deadlines when the action points will be undertaken. It also involves identifying the type of support one will need e.g. mentors and coaches.

Adopting and Routinizing Interventions

This is the actual implementation and reinforcement of the action points. The individual tries out the new behaviours he or she wishes to learn or to improve in order to achieve the goals. He or she looks for opportunities to try out the new behaviour. At this stage the individual learns from both the successes and failures of his or her efforts. Rewarding the individual in different ways for trying is important at this stage.

The next step is to transfer the new learning into the real life situation like at work or at home. Key to the success of this is to have an effective feedback system preferably with a speaking partner. The last step is to tie the new learning into one's identity. In an organizational setting, this may imply other changes like in the structure, culture and compensation systems.

While self -development is mostly an individual pursuit, it is necessary to identify a coach, mentor or speaking partner. For younger professionals, a speaking partner may be an admired mentor while for experienced professionals the speaking partner may be another trusted and experienced professional.

The role of the speaking partner is to provide feedback and support to the individual. Meetings are arranged at agreed frequencies to reflect on the achievement of the goals and objectives the individual is committing him or herself to and to plan for further goals, objectives and targets.

Individuals will be motivated to pursue their self-development in an environment, which is supportive to: the fulfillment of basic needs, protection and security to be able to experiment in a non-threatening environment; the use of groups in which people can develop a sense of belonging and acceptance and find their position, not on the basis of status or formal authority, but on the basis of their real wisdom, morality and skills in contributing and challenging people to develop their thinking and skills, and to take real responsibility.

Strategies for Self-Development

There are many ways of skinning a cat
Elders see while sitting, what the young may not
see standing on their toes
No matter how sharp a knife, it cannot cut itself

There is no one right way for pursuing the discipline of self-development. Different individuals and organizations follow different strategies and combinations of strategies. The three main strategies are: developmental Counselling, self-development workshops; and meditation programs.

Developmental Counselling

From our experience of working with organizations, we have observed that many leaders have deep professional and personal problems that they do not understand and do not know where to take to.

Developmental counselling is a process tailored for the individual to learn from his or her life experiences and practice and plan to improve his or her effectiveness. Developmental counselling is a regular, structured, prepared and focused session between an individual and an experienced and qualified speaking partner. The primary objective of developmental counselling is empowering individuals to undergo a process of self-evaluation, to become conscious of the hindrances of their own potential and then to take personal responsibility for developing their own capacities to achieve the goals and objectives they have set for themselves. Key questions guiding the process are: What goals and objectives did I set up for myself? How did I implement these goals and activities? What worked? What did not work? What lessons and insights did I get from the results? How can I use these insights in planning for further objectives and activities so that I can implement them at a higher level?

The most crucial point is on capturing lessons, learning and insights to enable one to let go of old ways of looking at things in order to take new learnings aboard. Developmental counselling is therefore aimed at being a tool for: self-appraisal process, guided self-discovery, achieving goals, personal encounter or self-confrontation and reinforcing success

Before the developmental counselling session, the individual reflects on the following questions and prepares a report that he or she gives to the speaking partner before the actual session:

1. What have I done over the period or since the last session? (a short summary)
2. What did I plan to achieve over the period?
3. What have I actually achieved?
4. What have I not achieved and why?
5. What went well?
6. Where did I have difficulty?
7. What can I learn from 3 & 4 above?
8. What are the new questions for me?
9. Developing a plan of what I want to achieve over the next period
10. What support or training may I need?
11. How am I feeling about what I am achieving in relation to my own personal objectives?

When the speaking partner gets the report, he or she prepares to give feedback to the individual. It is important that the speaking partner gets the report in good time so that he or she can have adequate time for in-depth thinking around specific issues, and coming up with developmental questions that will help provide new perspectives and challenge set ways of thinking and seeing things.

This works better when the report reaches the speaking partner at least two days before the scheduled session to allow time for the preparation.

During the actual session, the speaking partner gives some structure to the discussion so that it is focused and change oriented. Having an agreed amount of time for the session does this. When the session takes more than two hours, a break is recommended. A venue must be comfortable and facilitative to concentration. The agenda may look like:

1. Agree on the agenda, time and priorities
2. Any points from the previous sessions
3. Discussion around report
4. Summary of discussions
5. Planning for the next session
6. Evaluation of the session
7. Agreeing on the date, time and venue of the next session.

Developmental counselling may be quite expensive and is usually recommended in the following circumstances: Significant emotional disorder or interpersonal difficulties at home or at work, self-development directed toward working as a counsellor with others and difficult decision making connected with career or life planning where the person is faced with significant alternatives.

Self-Development Workshops

This program may be aimed at enabling individuals contribute more to their personal and organisational effectiveness by enabling them to tap more into their potential. The program enables individuals to discover themselves by helping them to: set up personal mission statements, align their careers to their missions, set personal goals and objectives, manage time effectively, clarify and adopt empowering values, master their mind– learn how to run their brains more effectively; and understand the role of mentoring in personal development

Self-development program workshops are aimed at raising one's understanding of the self, interpersonal processes and how to improve one's own and interpersonal competence. The program usually admits about 6 to 12 people at a time and facilitative training approach is adopted. Lectures must be minimized but most of the time is spent in reflective sessions. The workshops are ideally conducted away from the normal place of work. While organizations may have tailor made programs for their employees, the ideal situation is to bring together people from different backgrounds for maximum diversity. The diversity is ideal for learning as one is challenged to appreciate how others look at the world.

In-house programs should only be attempted in the following circumstances:

1. All members are genuine volunteers who understand the nature of the program and want to be involved.
2. The chief executive and at least some other senior executives are involved at the beginning.
3. Those who control the organization accept that the main aim of the group is Self-Development and that, while there may be organizational gains, there could also be organizational losses (e.g. a valuable employee may decide he wishes to pursue another career and resign).
4. Those involved are committed to observe confidentiality of personal material divulged in-group sessions.
5. There is an organizational commitment that personal material divulged in group sessions will not be taken into account in decisions affecting promotion, transfer, appraisal and dismissal.

To avoid such complications, organizations may find it easier to send their employees to external programs. The problem for external problems, however, is that the learning takes place outside the reality of the organization and as such there may be a mismatch between personal and organizational development. Those attending such programs may outpace the development of the organization resulting in individual-organization tensions. To address this challenge, the organization may do well to complement the external self-development programs with its own Organization Development (OD) program and team development initiatives.

Meditation

Based on the proverb, *what the eyes have seen the heart cannot forget*, meditation is the active engagement of the self to focus on a concern or an opportunity until it yields its secret. It is consciously working with a thought or a question until one 'squeezes every juice out of it'. Through meditation one strengthens the power of the intuition to give one insights that may not be available from the natural mind. Meditation requires a quiet place with no disturbances or distractions. Meditation works better with visualization of the thought, question or concern in the conscious mind and waiting quietly for guidance until one starts to notice movements of insight. The more one practices meditation the more the intuition is developed and the easier it becomes to get insights.

Intuition is the sense of the spirit that enables the individual to get direct perception of truth or fact independent of any natural reasoning process. Meditation therefore is learning by revelation and insight. It is indeed the highest form of learning. The development of intuition keeps one internally grounded and in tune with one's spirit or subconscious. Intuition gives inside guidance, advice, secrets, information and help on matters of importance to the individual e.g. on one's vision and purpose. If you consciously reflect on your purpose you will always provoke intuitive insight.

Meditation also enables one to observe processes using the mind. One can play a 'tape' on how he or she performed a certain task during the day or in some situation. The individual can relive the experience in the mind and take the role of an 'independent' observer. They can observe the process from the beginning to the end or backwards and they can play the tape again and again until it becomes and feels more and more real. After playing the tape, the individual can now reflect and learn from the experience on: what went well? What did not go well? What lessons and insights can be drawn? How could the process be done better next time? Meditation is difficult during first attempts but with frequent practice it becomes easier as the mind becomes more and more disciplined to be quiet and focus on a particular issue.

Another use of meditation is to create rhythm for mental and muscular relaxation. This is a form of stress management. While this is related to self-development, a good number of people have problems with it because of its religious overtones and its close links to Eastern religious practices like transcendental meditation like Yogi. We want to emphasize however that meditation is bigger than transcendental meditation and religion and for this reason those who are not comfortable with transcendental meditation must not throw away the bath water together with the baby. Everyone no matter their religious orientation can benefit from meditation practices that may be appropriate to them.

Conclusion

Peter Drucker's summarizes the essence of self-development in three statements: know your strengths, the first question to ask is what needs to be done rather that what one wants to do; and every six months ask yourself: what do I want to be remembered for? (Edersheim, 2007:13). Self-development is always about developing one's capacity with the aim of serving others.

In self-development, one's destiny is never determined by where one is coming from. *The wise aim at boundaries beyond the present; they transcend the parameters of their origins.*

Academic qualifications and experiences alone do not guarantee one's effectiveness as an individual. This explains why some individuals with very high academic qualifications may not be good leaders or managers. At the same time self-development does not substitute the need for academic development. But the argument is that in most organizations, there is more academic development as compared to self-development and that much of the current development approaches are still biased towards academics rather than self-development. This explains why in addition to academic qualifications, an individual must undergo self-development processes in order to become truly effective. Academic development and self-development are like two legs of an individual. They need each other. This is the way to true personal effectiveness– *the able blacksmith will lack no work.*

Enhancing Self-Development

What does the following proverb tell me about the importance of going through self-development processes?

A stream cannot rise above its source

What do the following proverbs tell me about my consciousness and that of my organization of the need for self-development as the foundation for our organisational effectiveness?

The greatest investment one can make is to invest in oneself
A self-controlled person is stronger that the person who can conquer many cities
A changed place cannot transform a person but a transformed person can change any place
One cannot know another person without first knowing oneself
There are no shortcuts to the top of a palm tree

How does the following proverb describe how well I respond to the different situations making demands on my life?

When the beat of the drum changes so must the step of the dance
The wise aim at boundaries beyond the present; they transcend the parameters of their origins

---

Chapter Three | Chiku Malunga
Organizational Wisdom in 100 African Proverbs (An Introduction to Organizational Paremiology)
London & Abuja, Adonis & Abbey Publishers

What do the following proverbs tell me about my need for continuous self-development process?

Life is like riding a bicycle; you don't fall off unless you stop pedaling

A person is taller than every mountain he or she has climbed

If a child washes his hands he will eat with kings

What do the following proverbs tell me about my need of a speaking partner or a mentor?

Elders see while sitting, what the young may not see while standing.

No matter how sharp a knife, it cannot cut itself

A barber does not shave himself

What strategies am I or is our organization using to implement self-development processes for individuals?

There are many ways of skinning a cat

CHAPTER FOUR

Relationships Development

There is nothing more important than relationships
It is better to be surrounded by people than to be surrounded by things

Introduction

All living systems are interconnected and interrelated. They are all interconnected and interrelated to form the one grand system called the universe. Any positive or negative impact on one system sends ripple effects to the entire universe. This is the basis of the saying; *one can do no evil but to oneself.* For the good of humanity and all forms of life a key word in all the systems is 'relationships'. The aim is to achieve a healthy equilibrium arrived at by mutually supporting relationships among the systems we have some control over. These harmonious relationships can be arrived at through efforts aimed at enhancing team spirit, managing conflict and promoting positive politics.

In all conscious relationships, there is no higher principle than love. Love simply defined is what others have described as the 'golden rule' – 'do unto others what you would like them to do for you'. This principle of love cannot be divorced from spiritual consciousness because it normally takes more than human will and effort to make it practical in day to day life. The 'self-preservation' instinct usually comes in the way of effective implementation of the 'golden rule'.

Individuals going through self-development processes are better able to create and manage healthy organizational relationships, which is a foundation for organizational effectiveness. In ensuring organizational effectiveness, *there is nothing more important than healthy relationships.* Effective organizations work through high performing teams. Wherever there is a group of people however, conflict is inevitable. Effective organizations find ways of keeping conflict at manageable levels. They also promote positive rather than negative organizational politics.

This chapter will discuss how organizations can ensure healthy relationships among the people in the organization through developing teams and team spirit, managing conflict and managing power and organizational politics. The chapter will also discuss how to ensure effective inter-organizational relationships.

Team Development

One man cannot move a mountain
No matter how powerful, one man cannot make rain fall on his farm only
Knowledge is like a baobab tree, no one person can embrace it alone
Ants united will drive a dead elephant to their abode
A bundle cannot be fastened with one hand

The goal of team development is to enable people in a group to function as a whole. This ensures that the people have a commonality of direction and that individuals' energies are harmonized and harnessed resulting in synergy. Such people share the vision and purpose of the group and they understand how they can complement one another's efforts.

A key change in transitioning from the first to the second phase of organizational development is the shift in emphasis from people as individuals to the roles they play. People are no longer called by their names but rather by their positions. Slowly the warm feelings of family vanish. The atmosphere of friendship gives way to an atmosphere of business. The organization is departmentalized. People are boxed into their offices, often with doors closed and their title posted. They briefly greet one another when they arrive at work and then close themselves in their offices. At this stage, it becomes very difficult for staff to focus at the people the organization serves because they may be busy looking after themselves. The organization may stop being responsive and becomes inward rather than outward looking. Many African and other bureaucratic institutions are clear examples.

When the human touch is lost for a long time, feelings of alienation and meaninglessness set in. Work becomes mechanistic. There is a genuine longing for "the old good days" but the laws of development dictates that we cannot go backwards. This plunges the organization into a major crisis, which is a cry for release of the human spirit in the mechanistic organization. The major motivation for the transition to the third phase is the realization that *one head cannot carry an entire roof alone* and that *friendship means adding value*. The next phase is characterized by a lot of team spirit and teamwork. The organization's main characteristics at this stage are a combination of those in the first and second phases. The walls separating the offices are broken down and people are put together again. Relationships are synergistic and adult-to-adult in nature. Work is organized by effective teams and task forces comprised of individuals from different departments and positions and exhibiting the characteristics below. There is a greater appreciation of the fact that, *"when cobwebs unite, they can tie up a lion"*.

So, we see the progression from dependence to independence to interdependence. It is indeed this matured stage of development that very few teams and organizations ever reach. Most remain stuck in the independent phase. It is in this last stage where friendship becomes added value and they can effectively collaborate with other organizations. There is no mutuality in collaborating with a dependent or non-responsive organization.

Characteristics of an Effective Team

CRITERIA	EXPLANATION
1. Clear Purpose	The vision, mission, goal, or task of the team is defined and accepted by everyone. There is an action plan
2. Informality	The climate is informal, comfortable and relaxed. There are no obvious tensions or signs of boredom
3. Participation	There is active discussion and everyone is encouraged to participate
4. Listening	The members use effective listening techniques such as questioning, paraphrasing and summarizing to get ideas
5. Civilized disagreement	The team is comfortable with disagreement, when it arises, and shows no sign of avoiding, smoothing over or suppressing conflict
6. Consensus decisions	Important decisions are made through substantial, if not unanimous agreement following open discussion of everyone's ideas, avoidance of formal voting or easy compromises
7. Open communication	Team members feel free to express feelings about tasks as well as group operations. There are few hidden agendas. Communication takes place outside of meetings.
8. Clear roles & work assignments	There are clear expectations about the roles played by each team member. When action is taken, clear assignments are distributed among the team members.
9. Shared leadership	While the team has a formal leader, leadership functions shift from time to time depending on the circumstances, the needs of the group and skills of the members. The formal leader models

	appropriate behaviour and helps establish positive norms
10. External relations	The team spends time developing key external relationships, mobilizing resources and building credibility with important players in the other parts of the organization
11. Style diversity	The team has a broad spectrum of team player types, including members who emphasize attention to task goal setting, focus on process and those who question how the team is functioning
12. Self-assessment	Periodically, the team stops to examine how well it is functioning and what may be hindering its effectiveness

Source: Parker 1990

We have found helping teams and organizations to create periodic sessions to reflect on the above description of an effective team, assessing itself and committing to take corrective action to be enough in strengthening teams within the organizations.

Another method for strengthening team spirit we have found to be effective is learning sessions or reflection periods. These help people in the organization not only to learn from their activities but also to reconnect with one another and cultivate team spirit. This is why such periods or moments must be spiced with a lot of fun. Conducting the reflection and learning sessions away from the office, having games and meals together and if possible and affordable allowing members of staff to come along with their spouses and families are some of the ways to achieve this. In one organization, they used to spend two days every twelfth week in reflection and learning. They called those two days *'back to the nest'* days. On those days all field and office work was suspended and every one was supposed to be at the 'nest' reflecting and learning and having fun.

Each organization must work out what is appropriate in their context. A rule of the thumb is that the reflection periods must not be too far apart and again they must not be too near each other. When they are too far apart, people may not remember what was learnt and the team spirit may not be sustained and when they are too near the reflection periods may cause paralysis.

Conflict Management

There is no venom like that of the tongue
A cutting word is worse than a bowstring; a cut may heal but the cut of the tongue does not
A word before it is uttered belongs to you; once spoken it does not
Where two rivers meet, the waters are never calm
You cannot kill the rat when it is on your clay pot

Just as *there is not a river that flows without a sound*, that is to say every home has its quarrels; conflict at manageable levels in organizations is normal and may even be an indicator of a healthy functioning organization. *Where two rivers meet, the waters are never calm.* Conflict at manageable levels may also be necessary because, *if two wise men agree on every point, there may be no need for one of them.* Conflict becomes a concern when it begins to have negative effects on organisational performance. The transition from the pioneer phase to the independent phase can have great negative implications for relationships in the organization if it is not well handled because it touches on organisational power dynamics. The predominant sources of power in the pioneer phase are charisma and connection. Charismatic leaders are able to influence others through their magnetic personalities. People close to the leader in turn derive power from their connection to the leader. Together, they usually also have the power to reward or punish others.

In the independent phase of the organization the sources of power that are emphasized are information, expertise and legitimacy. The move to the independent phase symbolizes a move towards professionalism. Since the people in the first phase were chosen on friendship ties more than on merit, they may not have the professional qualifications and experiences required to sustain their power in the new phase. This might require that new people with those qualifications and experiences be hired. The interplay of power sources between the 'veterans' and the newcomers can be a major source of conflict in the organization as the veterans defend their territories and the newcomers try to get their rightful positions in the organizations.

Conflict in the organization may occur at three levels: intra-personal, inter-personal; and inter-departmental. At the intra-personal level, individuals (especially veterans) may fail to come to terms with the current realities and prefer "the old good days". They may not understand why they suddenly have to account for every expenditure they make, why they can no longer use the organisational vehicle for personal use and why they cannot simply walk into the director's office without an appointment. The new comers may not understand why their qualifications are 'deliberately' not being recognized. They may not understand why their 'lack of experience' is such a big issue.

At the inter-personal level, conflict is normally between those who used to be powerful and those who are becoming powerful. For example, a clinical staff may develop conflict with a new doctor. Similarly, there is often conflict between experience and qualifications. The veterans may be more experienced but have fewer qualifications while the reverse may be true for the newcomers. Preference given to one group may generate resentment from the other. As a result, these two groups may not work together well.

At departmental level, conflict happens between different departments in the organization. The transition from dependent phase to independent phase may imply a change in priorities of the activities of the organization. This transition often implies more emphasis on the field activities of the organization. Actually, more and more donors are keen to fund activities and not administrative costs. While in the first phase the project departments and administrative departments might have been receiving the same attention, the shift to more emphasis on project staff may be a source of strained relationships between the project departments and administrative departments for example.

Conflict may also happen at intra-organisational level. The whole organization may be in conflict with itself often without fully knowing it. This often happens when there is a mismatch between what the organization does and what its task environment is asking of the organization. This is often manifested through the organization's collective efforts and achievement not matching. There is often more effort as compared to achievement. It is also manifested through general frustration among the people in the organization. Unfortunately, people in the organization may spend their time pointing fingers of blame at each other without realizing that such a conflict is a call for the organization to introspect and re-examine its vision, mission and strategies.

Conflict in the organization may take different forms. The form of the conflict is an indicator of how it can be resolved. Conflict may arise over: resource use, facts, structure, methods followed in doing work and values.

Conflicts arising out of scrutiny over use of inadequate resources may result in strained relationships at all levels described above. This type of conflict is the easiest to resolve because it implies getting more resources. When the resources have been provided, the conflict will go away.

Another type of conflict is over facts, e.g. how much in assets or money the organization has. People who do not know what they need to know become suspicious. When people argue over whether the direction is north or east the best way to resolve the conflict is to give them a compass. In a conflict over facts, therefore, the easiest way to resolve the conflict is to provide regular, objective information to the people concerned, such as statements of accounts, financial reports, project performance reports, and asset registers.

The structure of the organization may be another source of conflict. This is most often the case in situations where structures are formed before the strategic planning process. People may fight for space. Others may do more than they are supposed to while others do less. Others may be there who should not be there in the first place. The structure of the organization also shows people how they are supposed to relate to one another. When individuals are not comfortable in their positions, their relationships are negatively affected. Resolving this conflict involves redesigning and restructuring the organization to ensure that form follows function.

The fourth type of conflict is over work methods. Individuals with different methods may develop conflict over the right method for carrying out an assignment. While the organization should have a general approach to how it does its work, which provides a general framework for monitoring and evaluation, it must recognize that there is always more than one way of skinning a cat. Individuals, especially professionals must be given the freedom to use their discretion. Results and not methods must measure them as long as the methods fit within the general organisational approach and framework.

The last type of conflict is conflict over values. Values are the deep-seated beliefs regarding what is right or wrong; what is important and not important. Values form individuals' mental models and ways of looking at the world. Everyone believes that his or her way of looking at the world and things is right. We, therefore, tend to agree with those who look at the world and think like us and develop conflicts with those who do not. As systems of diversity, conflict is inevitable within organizations. The veterans may have different values from the newcomers. The newcomers may view the veterans as being conservative and having dictatorial tendencies while the veterans may view the newcomers as not very serious or not understanding how much they suffered to get the organization where it is today.

Conflict at values level is the most difficult to resolve as witnessed globally through wars, divorces, divisions in political parties and churches, etc. The best way to resolve this type of conflict is to prevent it from happening. Once it reaches a critical stage it is almost impossible to reverse. Helping individuals to change mental attitudes and be able to appreciate things from another's point of view is to gain the capacity for empathy, a valuable skill for resolving conflict.

The key principle to helping parties in conflict is to maintain objectivity and neutrality. The proverb *you cannot kill the rat when it is on your clay pot* means that conflict mediators cannot effectively help the parties in conflict when they are too close or have contributed to the conflict. To an organization, this means that leaders may be able to resolve some conflicts but may not be able to resolve others. Knowing which is which takes maturity. It is far easier for leaders to intervene in conflicts of resources or facts and increasingly more difficult in conflicts of methods, structure and values. Everyone in the organization is involved in the latter, which makes it difficult to maintain objectivity. External support is usually needed.

We have found the method below to be effective in helping groups in conflict:

In conflict management and resolution people will only change when they own the problem underlying the conflict and they see how they have contributed to the conflict personally. This means that for conflict to be truly resolved people must be brought to a contradiction between what they believe they are and what they truly are. This often involves bringing the 'warring' factions together and letting them go through a personal 'confession' process, which might look like this:

- Do you believe that there is conflict between the groups?
- If yes what type of conflict is it? (Intra-personal, inter-personal, inter-departmental, intra-organizational, etc?)
- What are the underlying causes of the conflict? (Resource use, Facts, Structure, Methods followed in doing work or Values)
- How did you personally contribute to the conflict (what did you commit or omit)?
- What commitment are you making towards resolving this conflict?

At the end of the session, the consultant summarizes the commitments and helps the group to come up with a 'healing process' action plan that specifies the agreed actions intended to heal the wounds caused by the conflict. This approach ensures that the consultant maintains his or her being perceived as a neutral player in the conflict.

Power and Politics in Organizations

Those who live in peace work for it
We make war so that we can live in peace
No matter how blunt, a machete should never be held by a mad person
You can order around a wild cat only if you have some chickens
One cannot do evil but to oneself
Negotiate with your enemy while you are strong and a formidable force, and he will always fear and respect you; but negotiate at the brink of defeat, and he will trample you down

Organizations are made up of people and discussing them can never be complete without talking about power and politics. Power and politics represent organizational realities. Conflict in any group is inevitable. Up to certain levels, conflict is a sign of organizational health as the proverb *we make war so that we can live in peace* suggests.

People in any group like to have influence on others. Everyone wants to feel more powerful and important. Put very simply, power is an individual's capacity to influence organizational outcomes. Power is the ability to get what one wants from the organization. In most organizations, the formal structure is rarely the real structure. The real structure is the one that is shaped by the exercise of power and politics in the organization.

It is the exercise of power that makes organizational life possible. Organizations cannot function without power to influence behaviour. Leadership and power are, therefore, closely related. Power helps individuals satisfy both personal and organizational objectives.

Types of Power and Politics in Organizations

There are two faces of power: positive and negative. On its own, power is neither positive nor negative. It is neutral. It is how power is used that makes it positive or negative. Positive power is aimed at inspiring, influencing and leading. It enables people to reach their goals. It seeks the mutual benefit and satisfaction of all. Negative power on the contrary is aimed at dominating others. Those using power in this way aim to meet their own goals and objectives at the expense of others. George Orwell's two books *Animal Farm* (1945) and *Nineteen Eighty Four* (1949) are examples of the practice of negative power. Positive power yields both acceptance and respect for the person practicing it. Negative power yields neither genuine acceptance nor respect. Negative power rules by manipulating and instilling fear in followers.

Bases of Power

According to Raven (1959), Raven & Kruglanski (1975) and Natemeyer (1979) there are seven main bases of power for individuals in organizations. Bases of power are the resource in one's possession that one can use to influence organizational outcomes in one's interest - *You can order around a wild cat only if you have some chickens.* The bases of power include:

1. *Reward Power–* based on the ability of the power-holder to reward or give something valued by the other. The person who can award promotions, for example, has power over the people to whom he can offer the promotions.
2. *Coercive Power–* based on the ability of the power-holder to punish or give something of negative value. The person with the authority to fire staff has power over those people.
3. *Legitimate Power–* based on people's belief that the power-holder has a legitimate right to exercise power and that those people upon whom the power is exercised have an obligation

to accept its influence. The psychological distance between the power-holder and the subordinates reinforces this power.

4. *Connection Power*– based on the power-receiver's connection to the power-giver. A secretary may be more powerful than officers because of his or her connection to the director.
5. *Expert Power*– based on the power-holder's expert knowledge or expertise needed by others. Your expertise may be necessary for another person to do his or her job satisfactorily – therefore, the person complies with your desires in order to benefit from your expertise.
6. *Information Power*– Closely related to expert power is information power. If your ability to influence the behaviour of someone is based on information you possess or have access to, you have an information power base. As with an expert power base, the information you have or can obtain may be so valuable to another person's job or prestige that he or she is willing to comply with your wishes in order to receive the information.
7. *Referent Power*– If your ability to influence the behaviour of another person is based on your personal traits, you possess referent power. You are so admired for your personal qualities – perhaps for charisma – that others want to be identified with you. They are willing to pay for a close association with you, and you thus wield power over them.

People involved in any organization – shareholders, donors, customers, clients, board members, management, etc. - have varying degrees of power over the outcomes of the organization. Often their interests are in conflict. Getting one's interests met over others' involves the use of power; called organizational politics. Organizational politics is based on the law of 'enlightened self-interest', which states: *In the long run people can be counted to do only what will be of great personal benefit to themselves, individually.* Organizational politics is played out in decision-making, resource allocation and conflict resolution processes. Politics, like power, can be either positive or negative depending on its use. Positive politics is found where there is a balance between individual self-interest and the interests of others, requiring a win-win philosophy. Negative politics is the extreme pursuit of self-interest, requiring a win-lose philosophy. The latter type rules by domination and instilling fear in people.

In most organizations negative politics is exercised through:

- *Controlling Information and Secrecy* – juniors may hide or withhold information that other groups or top management may require. In one case, old plumbers of a Water Service Organization avoided retirement by refusing to disclose the water pipe configuration. They were the only ones around when the water supply system was installed and no proper records had been kept on the system's design.
- *Denying the Competence of Outsiders* – A department may say that other groups are not as professional as themselves and that they have the real answers about the organization. In NGOs, this is often common between core and support staff. Some groups create myths around their professions and qualifications, such as, "lawyers working in organizations are always paid highly and therefore we must also be paid highly in this organization".
- *Distorting Information* – Individuals may distort information to enhance their image and diminish that of others by manipulating facts or submitting partial reports.
- *Formal Policies, Systems and Procedures* –Those in position of influence may impose self-serving policies to frustrate the other groups, similar to parliaments changing national constitutions to serve a few individuals in the ruling party. Such policies are often aimed at reducing the other groups' space while increasing your own. Those in positions of power may advocate for policies that will ensure the recruitment of like-minded people to reinforce their own power. This may

mean recruiting people who attended the same college or recruiting friends or relatives, for example.
- *Informal Policies, Systems and Procedures* – Individuals or groups that feel 'attacked' by formal policies, systems and procedures will usually find 'legitimate' or justifiable ways of getting around the imposed rules. They may create a 'fifth column' within the group formulating the restrictive policies to siphon information and remain a step ahead of that group.
- *Non-Cooperation* - One may frustrate another group by simply not co-operating. They may unkindly reject or criticize reports or deliberately do something wrong and say that the orders were not clear. The most common examples of this are strikes, go slows and sit-ins.

Increasing One's Power in an Organization

It is important to consciously work at increasing one's power – the positive face of power in the organization. This is because, as the proverb put its - *Negotiate with your enemy while you are strong and a formidable force, and he will always fear and respect you; but negotiate at the brink of defeat, and he will trample you down.*

There are a few tactics one can use to increase one's own power and exercise positive politics in an organization. Few of these are:

1. Working in such a way that one exceeds the expectations of both superiors and subordinates;
2. Helping others solve difficult problems and providing critical information;
3. Making oneself known to people with greater power;
4. Confronting others with caution and avoiding creating enemies;
5. Developing contacts with people outside the organization who have great influence on the organization, e.g., key customers, friends and relatives of the boss, board members, etc.;
6. Being supportive of causes advocated by those in authority;

7. Being loyal to both those above and below you;
8. Seeking counsel and advice from influential sources, especially those above you;
9. Being a person of integrity; being trustworthy and confidential, never betraying information;
10. Learning to use the organization and its policies to accomplish individual goals.

A key responsibility for leadership in any organization is to encourage positive politics - *those who live in peace work for it* and discourage negative politics by emphasizing that *one cannot do evil but to oneself*. It is also the responsibility of leadership to ensure that power or key positions in the organization are given to responsible people because *no matter how blunt, a machete should never be held by a mad person*.

Trans-organizational Development (TD)

No matter how powerful, one man cannot make rain fall on his farm alone

A related relationship building intervention is called trans-organizational development (TD). TD involves getting more than one organization or getting a number of stakeholders to 'work together collaboratively towards a common goal or objectives'. Peter Drucker rightly observes when he states, "it doesn't matter what your discipline is or how sophisticated you are technically. If you can't learn how to respect people and how to develop and nurture relationships, you can't reach your potential as an individual or company. No body works alone anymore at anything" (Edersheim, 2007: 155).

TD is useful in establishing and managing networks, business alliances or consortia formed with the aim of creating synergy among the organizations involved. TD is based on the principle that no matter how strong no organization can be self-sufficient in the sense of not needing the support of other organizations to achieve its goals.

'Synergy' therefore is the key word in TD. Organizations network to implement joint projects, share information and experiences and organize joint events among other reasons.

The TD process involves four main phases. These are:

1. Identifying Potential Members – The main activities of the TD practitioner are to help the people with the idea of forming the 'network' to form a steering committee and establish the preliminary membership criteria. He or she may also facilitate the induction of new members into the network.
2. Bringing together the member organizations – The TD practitioner facilitates a workshop for representatives of the member organizations to agree on the necessity of forming the network. This session enables the members to clarify their member expectations and fears. Much more importantly, the TD practitioner must help the members to agree on working values for the 'network'. Many networks fail because of unshared expectations and values among the members.
3. Establishing the Network - After agreeing on the purpose and generating enough energy and enthusiasm, the TD practitioner helps the members to create and agree on the ground rules, roles and responsibilities, decision making processes, communication mechanisms, an appropriate structure and on ways to secure the required financial and material resources. Most importantly, the TD practitioners help the members to agree on how the network will be coordinated.
4. A key role that a TD practitioner plays is to facilitate periodic reflection sessions on how the 'network' is doing. The TD practitioner helps the members to identify their successes and challenges and what they are learning from these. More importantly, how they can use the lessons to improve the performance of the network.

The TD practitioner may require much more 'energy' as much of his or her work will be to facilitate 'power-sharing and political interventions' especially at the beginning of the process. Being seen to be neutral and not taking sides is key to success in such interventions.

Conclusion

This chapter has discussed how organizations can ensure healthy relationships among the people in the organization through developing teams and team spirit, managing conflict and managing power and organizational politics. It has also discussed how to ensure effective inter-organisational relationships.

There is nothing more important than healthy relationships. Effective organizations work through high performing teams. Wherever there is a group of people, conflict is inevitable. Effective organizations find ways of keeping conflict at manageable levels. They also promote positive rather than negative organizational politics. In relationships, there is *no good that one does but to him/herself and there is no evil that one does but to him or herself. Ashes fly back into the face of the person who throws them.* Nothing is more important than relationships.

Building Relationships

How do the following proverbs discuss the team spirit and team development in our organization?

> *One man cannot move a mountain*
> *No matter how powerful, one man cannot make rain fall on his farm only*
> *Knowledge is like a baobab tree no one person can embrace it alone*
> *Ants united will drive a dead elephant to their abode*
> *A bundle cannot be fastened with one hand*

What do the following proverbs say about conflict and how it is managed in our organization?

There is no venom like that of the tongue
A cutting word is worse than a bowstring; a cut may heal but the cut of the tongue does not
Where two rivers meet, the waters are never calm
A word before it is uttered belongs to you; once spoken it does not
You cannot kill the rat when it is on your clay pot

How do the following proverbs describe power and politics in our organization?

Those who live in peace work for it
We make war so that we can live in peace
No matter how blunt a machete, it should never be held by a mad person
One cannot do evil but to oneself
Negotiate with your enemy while you are strong and a formidable force, and he will always fear and respect you; but negotiate at the brink of defeat, and he will trample you down

How does the following proverb describe people's consciousness of sources of power and how well these are being used?

Use what you have to get what you want
You can order around a wild cat only if you have some chickens

How does the following proverb describe how we are currently working with other organizations and other stakeholders?

No matter how powerful, one man cannot make rain fall on his farm alone

CHAPTER FIVE

Strategy, the Art of Creating the Future We Want

Tomorrow belongs to the people who prepare for it today
Prepare now for the solutions of tomorrow
Strategy is better than strength
The lion does not turn around when small dogs bark at it

Introduction

All living systems are subjected to the law of the survival of the fittest. Nature punishes the weak and rewards the strong. Over thousands of years the different species have developed survival mechanisms to perpetuate themselves. In order to survive and if possible thrive, a system must be relevant. Being relevant means being needed. If it is relevant the task environment will legitimize it by rewarding it with the resources it needs for its survival. For as long as it remains relevant and therefore needed, it will not be starved. In this way, the system and its benefits will be sustainable.

A system that is not relevant will be starved of the resources it needs for its survival. It will eventually sink into oblivion and become extinct. Dinosaurs became extinct because they could not adapt to a changing environment and therefore became irrelevant, unneeded and they starved to extinction. First and foremost, strategic planning is aimed at consciously and continually making the organization relevant to its current and emerging task environment. Only those organizations that are relevant are rewarded by the task environment for their sustenance because they are needed. Organizations that are irrelevant simply become extinct in the real sense of the word. All natural systems, organizations included, follow the law of the jungle – 'the survival of the fittest'.

Strategy is to an organization what self-development is to an individual. The principles are the same except that instead of dealing with an individual, we are now dealing with an entire organization as an entity. According to Covey (2004:248) a strategic plan is a crisp description of how you will provide value to your customers and stakeholders. It is your value proposition. It is your focus. It is the organization's focus (Covey, 2004:248). Strategy is about identifying what is important in the long term for the organization. *Like the lion that does not turn around when small dogs bark at it*, the organization must focus on its important and long term priorities and not be distracted by smaller or short term opportunities and challenges. In this way, the organization prepares itself for tomorrow today. In coming up with long term priorities, the organization also positions itself in relation to its competitors and collaborators in the task environment. Positioning implies proactively responding to the changing factors in the task environment and within the organization itself. *When the beat of the drum changes, so must the step of the dance.* It is important to note that strategic planning is not about the future. It is about how we should behave today to deserve the future we want. *If you really want to go to mount Olympus make sure that every step you make takes you nearer there.* Strategic planning is about creating a destination and making sure that every step we make takes us nearer that destination.

This chapter discusses the importance of strategic positioning for organizations. It discusses the strategic planning process and characteristics of effective strategies. It finally discusses the importance of linking organisational activities to the strategic plan of the organization.

Today, it is agreed that for organizations to survive in this difficult and competitive environment, they must have an effective strategic plan. A good plan stipulates the organization's niche and clearly outlines strategies to employ to capitalize on its niche. Financially, an effective strategic plan enables an organization to understand the minds of those who can give it the money it needs. It informs staff how to organize in order to attract needed resources. A strategic plan also enables the organization to look seriously at what resources they already have and how well these are being used. In non-profit organizations for example, because of the belief that, "donors will give us money", many organizations greatly underutilize the resources they already have. One has just to look at the many vehicles in government departments that have been parked for minor faults simply because, "a donor will give us another one". Sustainability means becoming increasingly self-reliant and making the best use of what we have to reduce dependency on external support.

Strategic Positioning: The Goal of Strategic Planning

A mother of twins must sleep on her back
The sun shines on those standing before it shines on those sitting
When a baobab tree has fallen, the goats start climbing on it.

A mother of twins must sleep on her back so that she can breast feed her twins more conveniently and effectively. Similarly, every organization needs to strategically position itself to serve its constituents more effectively. Strategic positioning involves creating a vision and translating the vision to action. It involves turning vision into reality.

Creating a vision is one thing and translating the vision into tangible activities on the ground is another. The process of translating vision into activities is called strategic planning. The actual turning of vision into reality is called strategic work. Two organizations may share the same vision but the one with the most effective strategy will achieve the most impact. Strategic planning answers how the vision will be implemented and managed in the organization.

The strategic plan enables the organization to build on its strengths, take advantage of opportunities and address threats in the task environment. Strategic planning enables the organization to consciously respond to the changes taking place both inside and outside of the organization and influence these changes as much as possible. The aim of strategic planning is to prepare today's organization for tomorrow because *failing to plan is planning to fail.*

Two major benefits of a strategic plan are: (1) the planning process is a learning process for all involved: the board members, members of staff and the other stakeholders and (2) the plan document becomes a management and a governance tool for the management and the board respectively. As a learning process, strategic planning and management enhances the capacity of the organization to adapt and manage change.

Positioning means how we want to be ranked among organizations doing the same things we are doing. There may be for example 10 organizations doing similar things. Out of that group of 10, how do we want to be ranked? Do we want to be number one, number two or number five for example? What is our ranking today? What is it going to take us to reach the ranking that we want?

For a long time, we have been told that Africa is the poorest continent among the continents. That may be where we are today but is it where we want to be? Our level of seriousness to move to a higher rank will be measured by our strategic capacity – the ability to identify how we want to be ranked and doing all and anything it takes to actually move to the desired rank.

Uniqueness

The essence of strategic planning is in identifying and cultivating an organization's uniqueness – that which sets the organization apart from all others. *If lizard meat was good there wouldn't be so many lizards around.* It is only the good meat that is in demand. It is in demand because it is good. It is unique. In organizational and individual life, uniqueness results from innovation and creativity. It arises from providing completely different products or services. It can also arise from providing similar products and services in significantly different ways.

Uniqueness is what attracts to the organization all the opportunities and resources it needs. Husain Bolt is a very rich man because he is the fastest man on earth. Uniqueness equals wealth. No truly unique person or organization can be poor. *The able blacksmith will never lack work.* Bob Marley is one of the richest dead musicians because his music was unique. Genuine individual and organizational uniqueness gives an organization or the person 'staying power'. Sometimes even beyond death. Achievements arising from uniqueness cannot be erased.

A key indicator of lack of uniqueness is poverty. Poverty is so prevalent because the majority of the people are not unique. There is no competition for a truly unique person or organization.

AFRICAN PROVERBS STRATEGIC THINKING SELF-ASSESSMENT TOOL

Rating (0 –5): 0 = we do not experience this in our organization
5 = we strongly experience or observe this in our organization
Rate yourself and explain why you give yourself that rate.

Rate 0- 5   0 = Non – existent   5 = Excellent

1. How conscious is our organization on the importance making lasting impact and leaving a strong legacy?
   -*Every one dies but not everyone lives.*
   -*All people die but not all are buried*
   -*Lions don't die, they just sleep.*
2. How well is the organization able to forecast possible future scenarios and plan based on the scenarios?
   -*You can only jump over a ditch only if you can see it from afar.*
3. How well has our organization identified and strives to remain within its niche so that it maximizes its impact and minimizes competition?
   -*A cat in his house has the teeth of a lion.*
4. How consciously has our organization made the following strategic decisions and adheres to them to ensure focus and concentration?
   -Whether to be an implementer or facilitator.

> -Whether to cover a large geographical area or to focus an effort in a small area and expand gradually as we make impact.
> -Whether to offer many projects/services or just a few.
> -Whether to respond to root causes or symptoms (at what level of depth to intervene).
> -Whether to work in isolation or in collaboration.
> -Whether to take a short term or long term approach.
> -*At the crossroad you cannot go in both directions at the same time.*
> -*If you run after two hares, you will catch neither*
> 5. How consciously does our organization pace the implementation of its strategy so that resources and capacity constraints do not become a bottleneck?
> -*More haste less speed.*
> -*No matter how hungry you are, you can only eat your meal one mouthful at a time.*
> 6. How regularly and consciously does our organization review its strategy to see if it is still relevant to the changing factors – the task environment? *When the beat of the drum changes, so much the step of its dance*

The Strategic Planning Process

Since men have learnt to shoot without missing, birds have learnt to fly without perching
There is no such a thing as bad weather, only bad clothing

The strategic planning process is the organization's proactive response to what the task environment is saying. It is an organization's response to the demands of its task environment for it to remain legitimate, relevant and sustainable. The response involves building its capacity to effectively respond to the opportunities and threats in the task environment arising from political, economic, technological and socio-cultural factors. The strategic planning process may take different forms and shapes depending on the type of the organization and the different contexts in which the organizations find themselves. But the general process is given below:

The Meaning of Vision

What the eyes have seen, the heart cannot forget

Vision is the ability to see beyond the present realities to a desired future. Vision crafting means creating the future the organization wants in people's minds and hearts. It is the strong sense of vision in an organization that creates developmental motion. Vision is the magnet in the future that pulls the organization in that direction. Vision is the organization's 'home' in the future. *No matter how far people are from their homes, they will keep moving in that direction until they get there.* Vision is what the organization wants to see changed in the society as a result of its existence and work - the 'seeing' results in heart commitment by all members of the organization.

Where there is no vision there is no heart. People must 'see' the vision of the organization in order to put their heart into the organization. Without vision, there is no unity of purpose. The organization becomes flaky, reduced to only a source of livelihood for the people inside. Where there is no vision, energy dissipates with the lack of focus or concentration. People in the organization become blind and deaf to what their task environment is telling them. They stop being responsive and become inward looking. They do not see the need for improvement as long as activities continue.

When the vision is clear and effectively communicated to the beneficiaries and all stakeholders (or created together with them) a sense of ownership and commitment is created. Many organizations do not take time to communicate their vision to beneficiaries and stakeholders, let alone create it with them. Instead, they go into communities with projects and activities. When people do not see the vision behind the activities and the projects, they cannot be transformed or committed, making it difficult for them to be self-organized for sustainability. The real work of leadership is to congruently communicate the organization's vision. Most of the failures in many organizations can be attributed to failure in communicating and entrenching the vision.

People tend to confuse a vision with a dream. A vision is the picture of the desired situation in our task environment and some realistic ideas on how it will be achieved. A dream may also be a picture of the ideal situation but without clear ideas and strategies to back it. A dream may be mere wishful thinking and fantasy. Many organizations do have vision statements, but unless they are believed and internalized they mean nothing. It is difficult to work with people who are sleeping or sleep walking because there is no consciousness to bring meaning to their activity. It is the articulation of the vision that brings about consciousness. Otherwise, the visions become mere dreams.

Organizational success may be accidental but all long lasting self-sustaining success is built on a strong and clear vision. There is no such a thing as luck. There is only cause and effect. Organizations, especially young ones, may not have a strategic plan but they cannot afford not to have a clear and strong vision – one that the eyes can see and the heart can be committed to.

The Organization's Mission

The strategic planning process starts with formulating mission based on the vision statement. The mission statement is a guiding star of the organization. It is the ultimate and real constitution for the organization and therefore the highest authority in the organization. It specifies the identity of the organization, the purpose, the target group and the values of the organization. It is important that an organization must clearly define whom it will be serving. This helps to focus and concentrate the efforts of the organization. Focus and concentration are important because *the dog that belongs to everyone in the village will die of starvation.*

It is a primary duty of organizational leaders to lead by example. Leaders must live and personify the values of the organization. This is important because *when a chief limps, all his subjects limp too.*

In implementing strategic plans, the major problem that many organizations, especially non-profit organizations face is not that the people are lazy or not committed to work. Many of them do not consciously link their organization's activities with their mission and strategies. They keep responding to every 'threat' and 'opportunity' in the task environment as if they were fighting wild fires. Organizations must make sure that their mission statements are adequately internalized and are consciously used as a guide for deciding which activities to pursue or not. At the same time, the mission statements must be wide enough to allow for flexibility as the organization navigates through emerging threats and opportunities in the task environment.

The next major steps in strategic planning are described below.

1. **Environmental Scanning**

If you can bear the hissing of a snake do not complain when you are bitten
A person's life is in his ears
Another person's misfortune should give you wisdom

Many times organizations are too slow to notice the changes that are taking place in the environment and to respond in time. As a result of this, they lose touch and they are negatively affected. They do not notice the grass growing around them until they are completely covered by bush.

Environmental scanning involves observing changes, trends and patterns in the task environment over a number of years in the past. The observations are made on the political, economic, socio-cultural technological factors that influence the organization's work. This also involves industry specific factors. Civil society organizations, for example, will be interested in the attitude of government toward human rights in the country, the effect of the economy on political decisions, the present and evolving human rights consciousness among the masses and the use of public print and electronic media, etc. In addition to studying these factors nationally, the organization may want to also understand what changes are affecting the geographic region, other countries or a specific industry or sector. The aim is to learn how organizations are being affected.

When the trends, changes and patterns have been established, the next step is to try to see what these say about what the future is likely to be. The ability to see what shape the future might take is a critical survival skill for organizations.

One has to see a ditch from afar to jump over it effectively

When a probable picture of the future over the next three to five years has been envisioned, it is put next to the vision and mission statements of the organization developed above. This helps identify the issues that the organization must address in its task environment. The juxtaposition indicates the amount and scope of work that organization will do.

An egg does not rot in one day

The work an organization can do is limited by its internal capacity. Therefore, the next step is to do an internal scanning to identify the changes, patterns and trends that have taken place inside the organization, which the organization may not have perceived. Internal scanning creates a picture of the current internal capacity (strengths and improvables) of the organization at present and some years in the future.

The internal picture is measured against the picture emerging from the external environmental scan. These bring out what the organization can realistically do now and what capacity gaps need to be addressed. *What is the point of having so much land when you have no capacity to utilize it?*

Since no organization is isolated from its environment and the other players in it, part of the scanning process involves identifying the key stakeholders, or those individuals and groups that are

Chapter Five | Chiku Malunga
Organizational Wisdom in 100 African Proverbs (An Introduction to Organizational Paremiology)
London & Abuja, Adonis & Abbey Publishers

interested either in the success or failure of the organization. Objectively, asking questions like, "Who would celebrate if we fail? Who would rejoice if we succeed?" "Whose help do we need to succeed?" would reveal the organization's main stakeholders. Next, the organization needs to find ways to strengthen relationships with its friends and win over its enemies and those we need for our success or minimize their negative effects.

2. **Identifying Issues to Address and Goals to Pursue**

If you cut a piece of a liana creeper plant without removing the roots it will continue to creep
When the tree falls the monkeys scatter
If you can't stop the monkeys from coming to the banana tree you cut down the banana tree

In order to effectively and proactively respond to both the internal and external environments, the organization must address fundamental issues rather than mere symptoms, which may exhaust the organization's energy without much results. The process involves digging deeply to understand the causes of the threats and the weaknesses. It also involves understanding the leverage points to build upon strengths inside the organization and recognize opportunities in the task environment.

The two pictures created in the previous step guide this process. The picture from the task environment scanning may look very complex but a proper analysis will reveal that there are only a few issues creating the complexities. Real leverage is found in identifying and addressing the actual issues creating the actual and emerging status quo. Poverty in communities, for example, may have its real source in policies governments and business are implementing and following rather than among the poor people themselves.

Drawing from the environmental scanning and guided by the mission statement, the organization draws out its goals and objectives. The major areas needing goals and objectives are:

- Marketing– making the people the organization serves know it and the uniqueness of its services and products, trust the organization, its knowledge and experience, like it among competitors and choose it among the competitors.
- Innovation– ability to adapt and invent for leverage. This is key for identifying and using the organizations uniqueness.
- Human Resources development and management –how the organization will attract, develop and retain the people it needs
- Financial resources– the financial and material resources the organization will need to effectively carry out its work
- Productive use of the resources –how well the organization will use the financial, material and human resources it has
- Social Responsibility– how the organization will (apart from through its normal activities) thank the community for supporting it
- Profit requirements (for profit making organizations) and impact (for nonprofit organizations)

3. Identifying Strategies

When the organization has developed its goals and objectives, it then agrees on the new strategies it will adopt in order to accomplish its mission. Organizations must consciously look for new and better ways of being and doing rather than believing that what we have been and what we have been doing will suffice. Many leaders find it difficult to let go of what is no longer working- may be because this is what they know best. But if we keep defending our yesterday, we cannot deserve our tomorrow.

A strategy is the most effective way for achieving a goal. It is a choice among alternatives. The factors listed below must be considered in choosing effective strategies.

Effective Strategies Ensure Focus and Concentration

Rays of light concentrated through a lens can set an entire forest ablaze
If you run after two hares at the same time you will catch none

Effective strategies concentrate on the niche of the organization in the task environment. It is only when we concentrate our resources of time, money and energy on a few carefully identified strategies that we can be assured of success. This type of concentration enables depth and impact.

Effective Strategies Must Identify and Utilize Leverage

A hunter with one arrow does not shoot with a careless aim
If you are not pretty, know how to sing
If you cannot be a butterfly in beauty, be an elephant in size
Strategy is better than strength

Effective strategies build the capacity of an organization to use minimum possible effort to make the maximum impact. They aim at pulling clients rather than pushing or forcing them to do what the people in the organization want. Effective strategies make the organization attractive to its stakeholders and compensate the shortcomings with strengths. Effective strategies enable the organization to do what needs to be done rather than doing what the people in the organization want to do.

Effective Strategies are Few

When you are at a crossroad you cannot go into both directions at the same time

Organizations must make critical choices based on their mandate, resources and capabilities. This enables the organization to make maximum impact within its limitations. This also guides the organization to narrow its strategies and accrue a few plausible ones. This is possible only when the organization is focused and knows its future direction and its ultimate destination.

Effective strategies aim to enable the people to foresee the future as much as possible. It enables people to create mental models in anticipation of different aspects of the organization and its activities in the future. This compels them to start acting so as to ensure its future existence that they deserve. This telescopic attitude is a critical success factor in an era where organizations are continually being shocked by unexpected changes that they could not foresee.

Effective Strategies Enable the Organization to Match its Work with its Capacity

What a duck has failed to pick, a chicken cannot pick
The dry grass should not challenge fire
A child can crush a snail but it cannot crush a tortoise
It was ignorance that made the mouse to challenge the cat to a wrestling match

Effective strategies enable the organization to balance its internal capacity and the amount of work it can undertake. Many organizations feel that if they have a lot of work they are being successful and add one project after another. Sometimes this is a survival mechanism, since more projects means more money. However, the money may flow in but the workload might be too much to handle efficiently and successfully. Effective strategies enable the organization to identify the few important projects that match the capacity of the organization. *No matter how hungry you are, you can only eat your food one mouthful at a time.*

4. Implementation

A lazy man's farm is the breeding ground for snakes
Pray for a good harvest but keep on hoeing
Success is a ladder that cannot be climbed with hands in your pocket
A wise person does not fight the river with both legs at the same time
No matter how hungry you are, you can only eat your meal one mouthful at a time
Take it easy with the drums the night is still long
Good intentions are like children crying in church; they should be carried out immediately

The strategic plan gives an idea of what we would want to harvest at the end of the day. But it is just a plan. The actual harvest will only come as a result of effective and well coordinated implementation. The strategies are implemented through activities, since without those strategies remain mere dreams.

Each strategy must be broken down into activities that we can start working on today. This will ensure their implementation. Strategic planning ends with action, which the leaders must lead and manage. Work must be clearly defined, assigned, monitored and evaluated.

A proper identification of the issues forms a guide to the goals that the organization must have. Issues brought forth from the task environment scanning form the basis for program and organisational goals. The issues coming from the internal organization audit forms the basis for organisational capacity building goals. After the goals have been identified, the next step is to identify how they will be realized. This implies identifying effective strategies.

If the process of moving from vision to goals to strategies has been done well, identification of activities, targets and indicators should be very easy. Targets and indicators measure performance. Targets describe what is to be achieved while indicators specify how to know that targets are being met. Indicators may appear at all the levels of the strategic planning process and they measure different things at each level. At the activities level they measure efficiency; at the strategies level they measure effectiveness; at the goals level they measure they measure impact; at the mission level they measure the legacy of the organization; and at the vision level they measure societal transformation.

The major challenge to the plan lies in how consciously it is implemented. Here are some common reasons for unsuccessful plans:

Strategic plans are not owned. Organizations, especially non -profit and public, are directed by donors to develop a strategic plan as a funding requirement, making it superficial;

Strategic plans are done without conviction of their importance. Many organizations undergo a planning process 'because the 3 years of the first strategic plan have come to an end';

Many organizations undergo strategic planning processes reactively and not proactively. Organizations call for a planning process when they have a big problem, such as their survival is threatened by lack of donors yet once they get money they rarely use the plan.

In addition to leading the change process implied by the strategic plan, Beckhard & Pritchard (1992: 69 –70) think that leaders must pay special attention to the transition that comes about as a result. They must pay special attention to: how the work will be managed; what structures are required for the tasks; how to ensure commitment and involvement by all people; how to ensure effective communication with stakeholders; and how to rely on internal and external expertise to manage the transitional and implementation processes.

Personal Performance Systems

Planning that is not translated into work is a waste of time and resources. If time, money, people and other resources are not committed to the plan, nothing will happen. Strategic plans must also be supported by personal performance systems. If the organization does not have a way of measuring the performance of its individuals and teams in relation to the demands of the strategic plan, chances are high that the strategic plan will not be effectively implemented. Conducting performance appraisals and monitoring and evaluation is a way of providing feedback to the strategic plan.

Conclusion

The future belongs to the people who prepare for it today and the *lion does not turn around when small dogs are barking at it.* Strategic planning is about preparing the organization for tomorrow by identifying what is important for the organization in the long term. Strategic planning therefore enables an organization to move towards its future with a strong sense of direction and purpose without being unnecessarily distracted by smaller opportunities, threats and the challenges of yesterday.

Strategy is not about what we will do in the future but what we need to do today to deserve the future we deserve. Our future is inherent in what we do today. What we do today must be informed by the future we envision. *If you want to know the way to a place you have never been, ask those who are coming from it.* The vision 'has been to the future we desire' and therefore can act as a guiding star to our destination.

Strategic Positioning

1. How do the following proverbs help us understand the importance of strategic planning

    The lion does not turn around when small dogs bark at it
    The future belongs to the people who prepare for it today
    Prepare now for the solutions of tomorrow
    Strategy is better than strength

2. How do the following proverbs describe the current strategic position of our organization?

A mother of twins must sleep on her back
The sun shines on those standing before it shines on those sitting
Since men have learnt to shoot without missing, birds have learnt to fly without perching
There is no such a thing as bad weather, only bad clothing
When a baobab tree has fallen, the goats start climbing on it

3. How does the following proverb describe our organizational vision?

What the eyes have seen, the heart cannot forget

4. How do the following proverbs describe how well we 'read' our task environment as an organization?

If you can bear the hissing of a snake do not complain when you are bitten
Another person's misfortune should give you wisdom

5. How do the following proverbs describe how well we are able to 'foresee' issues in the organization?

One has to see a ditch from far away to jump over it effectively

6. How do the following proverbs describe how conscious we are as an organization on the state of our internal organizational capacity?

An egg does not rot in one day

7. What do the following proverbs say about the depth of issues we are addressing as an organization?

If you cut a piece of a liana creeper plant without removing the roots it will continue to creep

When the tree falls the monkeys scatter

If you cannot stop the monkeys from coming to the banana tree you cut down the banana tree

8. What do the following proverbs say about the effectiveness of our strategies in terms of:

Identifying and utilizing leverage

A hunter with one arrow does not shoot with a careless aim

If you are not pretty, know how to sing

If you cannot be a butterfly in beauty, be an elephant in size

Number of strategies we are implementing

When you are at a crossroad you cannot go into both directions at the same time

Rays of light concentrated through a lens can set an entire forest ablaze

Matching our capacity to our workload or the challenges our organization wants to address in the task environment

What a duck has failed to pick, a chicken cannot pick

The dry grass shouldn't challenge fire (check if correction here is ok)

A child can crush a snail but it cannot crush a tortoise

It was ignorance that made the mouse to challenge the cat to a wrestling match

9. What do the following proverbs say about the way we are implementing our strategic plan?

A lazy man's farm is the breeding ground for snakes
Pray for a good harvest but keep on hoeing
Success is a ladder that cannot be climbed with hands in your pocket
A wise person does not fight the river with both legs at the same time
No matter how hungry you are, you can only eat your meal one mouthful at a time
Good intentions are like children crying in church; they should be carried out immediately
Take it easy with the drums the night is still long

CHAPTER SIX

Organizational Structure

Many hands make work lighter
If the sun says it is more powerful than the moon
then let it come and shine at night
The cat in his house has the teeth of a lion
A house is supported by its rafters big and small
A pole is strengthened by another pole

Introduction

All living systems are supported by a structure. The structure evolves from simplicity to complexity as the system grows and develops. The natural sequencing is unity to differentiation to integration. A plant starts with a seed. The seed differentiates into a root and shoot which later on further differentiates and integrates into more and deeper roots; and the stem, branches and fruits. The aim of the structure is to support the functions of the system. As the system grows and develops, its functions become more specialized, need a more elaborate structure. Just as animal life would be impossible without a skeleton, organizational life would be impossible without some form of a structure.

While *many hands make work lighter*, many times there are challenges on how the work will be divided especially as the organization is growing. This is the primary justification for organisational structure. Organizational structure clarifies what is expected of individuals and departments in the organization in terms of their work. The organization's vision describes what the people in the organization would want to see changed in their task environment as a result of their work. The mission defines the organization's specific contribution to this desired change. The strategy defines how the organization intends to accomplish its mission. In other words, the strategy defines the work the organization will be doing. Organizational structure defines how the people in the organization intend to 'divide the work among themselves'. The organizational structure is the basis for group and individual job descriptions. All key areas of responsibility must be assigned as *a calabash with holes cannot be filled* and also *a house is supported by its rafters, big and small.*

To be effective, the structure must facilitate and not hinder the implementation of the strategy. This chapter will discuss how to design an appropriate structure for an organization. Each organization must have a structure that is appropriate to its unique situation. Organizations must not steal or simply imitate other organizations' structures because, *"it isn't difficult to steal your friend's flute but how are you going to play it?"*

The Evolution of Organizational Structure

There are no short cuts to the top of a palm tree
A journey of a thousand miles started with one step

To be effective, the development of organizational structure must be organic. A seed when planted first differentiates into a root and a shoot. The roots develop and become more complex. The shoot develops into a trunk, branches and leaves. It finally develops fruits, which contain seeds to start the life cycle all over again. In a way, a single seed is a potential forest. Similarly, the human being grows from less to more and more complexity. The first 12 or so years are characterized by simplicity and dependency. Adolescence is characterized by questioning and a search for independence. Early adulthood is characterized by seeking synergy through marriage, family and work relationships among others.

In the above process, we see a movement from less to more complexity. We also see a movement from less to more effectiveness.

The organism is able to be and do more and more as it moves from its simple form to differentiation through integration.

Since we have already shown that organizations are natural systems and that they follow natural processes of growth and development, the development of structure in the organization must be organic. In other words, the structure that the organization adopts must correspond to its stage of development. New and young organizations may need a simple and informal structure. Established organizations may need a more formal structure. When the formal structure becomes a constraint, the organization may need a re-integration of the formal and informal aspects of structure. Contrary to common belief, the 'flat structure' may not be the only right way to structure an organization. See below the structural characteristics of an organization along the stages of development:

Dependent Stage:

- There is no clear recognized structure in the organization. The leader acts as a hub to which everyone is attached
- Roles and responsibilities among the individuals and departments are not clear
- There is a 'family' feeling in the organization

Independent Stage:

- The organization is hierarchical
- Clear roles and responsibilities
- Roles and responsibilities are fixed according to one's specialization
- Individuals and departments work independently
- Relationships are formal

Interdependent Stage:

- The organization is 'flat' and people work mostly through teams. It is an organization of 'equals'.

- The organization is responsible to changing needs in the environment and has the capacity to re-organize and renew itself
- Redefined and clear roles and responsibilities
- Roles and responsibilities are temporary and may change from time to time
- Individuals and departments collaborate
- Problems are solved by task forces composed of diverse professional skills
- The primary commitment of the individual is to the profession rather than the organization
- Leaders and managers work as coordinators between various temporary work teams
- The organization collaborates effectively with other stakeholders
- There are conscious team building efforts to ensure close and satisfying relationships

As seen from the above, overall, the most effective structure is the interdependent stage structure. But the paradox is that organizations cannot just arrive at this stage without passing through the independent stage. Development stages cannot be jumped. In most organisational literature and practice, there is a strong promotion for organizations to become 'flat'. We also observe among many organizations that try to artificially jump some stages being brought back to the stage they belong, causing much frustration to the efforts aimed at making the organization flat. Only those organizations, which are 'ready' to become flat, can truly become flat. People in organizations must understand at which stage of development they are and what structure would be more appropriate for them.

Conflicts between the formal and informal structure in organizations are often due to a mismatch between the adopted structure and the stage of development of the organization. This also explains the need for different groups in the organization to develop at the same pace. When one group develops at a faster pace than the other, the slower group holds the other group back. In many organizations, we observe the secretariat developing faster than the board for example. With the increasing need for accountability and transparency as a prerequisite for funding, more and more donors are requiring the involvement of a vibrant board in the grant making process. If the board is weak in this regard, it will hold back the overall development of the organization. Similarly, if the core staff are prioritized and developed more than support staff, the frustration and resentment from the latter will hold back the development of the whole organization.

In any organization, there are at least three organizational structures. These are the documented structure, the structure that actually works or the one actually being followed and the desired or ideal structure. Fortunate, and indeed rare, are those organizations in which all these structures are one. Organizational politics is the major explanation of the multiplicity of the structures in an organization. Those organizations practicing positive politics are more likely to have unified structures. Those practicing negative politics are likely to have more than one structures existing at the same time.

Factors Determining the Structure of an Organization

While the stage of development of the organization must be the major consideration in structuring an organization, there are other factors that will also determine the type of structure that the organization will adopt. Among these are:

Legal Requirements

The turtle would like to dance, but just doesn't have the legs

The form of registration the organization takes will determine the required legal structure of the organization. Registering under the trustees act will require that the organization have a board of governors and a secretariat. Registering as a company limited by guarantee will require that the organization have a board of directors. These legal requirements may be facilitative or hindering to the effectiveness of the organization. Forcing organizations in stage one to have separate boards and secretariats before they are ready may hinder their effectiveness. In this case like the turtle, the organization may want to have a different structure but the legal requirement may not allow it that freedom.

Expectations of the Wider Environment

All the stars shine but some shine brighter than others
When the beat of the drum changes so must the step of the dance

Stakeholders' expectations may determine the type of structure the organization will adopt. An organization may want to adopt a flat structure but the stakeholders may not 'allow' it. In one organization, they tried to have a 'directorless' organization in the name of making the organization flat but it did not work. They tried to have a rotating directorship, but it did not work either. The donors insisted that they needed to see one person taking the ultimate responsibility of the organization and that they did not like the rotating directorship because it undermined the organization's consistency in dealing with external stakeholders. While organizations may want to have 'flat' organizations, *'all the stars shine but some shine brighter than others'* may be a strong value in the environment making such arrangements (to have flat organizations) not possible. In some instances, however, the reverse may be true. The organization may want to hold on to bureaucratic and hierarchical modes but its task environment may demand otherwise.

Boards and Secretariat

Two fingers cannot enter into one nostril
A cat in his house has the teeth of a lion

One area that needs clear definition is the distinction between the boards and management in an organization. The board plays the governance role. Management plays the management role. The board and management together play the leadership role. See table below for the governance leadership and management tasks.

- The board plays the governance role. Governance is mostly concerned with formulating strategy and directing policy;
- The secretariat plays the management role. Management is mostly concerned with implementation of activities;
- Both the Board and Management play the leadership role. Leadership is mostly concerned with managing the vision of the organization. Since the leadership is shared between the board and the secretariat, the specific responsibilities of each must be negotiated otherwise there will be conflict between the two.

Table 3: The Governance, Leadership and Management Tasks

Governance	Leadership	Management
1. Custodians of the long-term vision	1. Establishes and communicates the long-term vision	1. Relating the long-term vision to current activities
2. Safeguard the mission and strategy and make sure management is in line	2. Translates the vision and strategy into achievable objectives	2. Translating the mission and strategy into activities
3. Appoint suitable people at senior levels in the organization	3. Inspire people to use their creativity	3. Ensuring people can do what is expected of them
4. Motivate management by giving praise where it is due	4. Develop staff and volunteers by example and team work	4. Seeking improvement through training, briefing, exchange visits etc.
5. Identify major performance	5. Creates	5. Establishing procedures and ensuring staff

problems 6. Focusing on the long term and making sure the organization is going in the right direction 7. Monitoring significant changes in the task environment	effective policies and systems 6. Focus on effectiveness through doing the right things 7. Look into the future and create opportunities	know them 6. Focus on efficiency and being economic - doing things right at minimum cost 7. Look at the present and take advantage of current opportunities and react appropriately to challenges

It is important for the board and management to know and respect their boundaries. This is because *the authority of the chief does not cross the river.*

The Board

When kings lose direction they become servants
If the sun says it is more powerful than the moon then let it come and shine at night
The fingers of the hand are all different but they are all important

When civil society organizations and other non-profit organizations are described as voluntary organizations, this refers to the board. As opposed to the paid staff, the board has no self-interest in organization's funding because it does not affect their purse. Donors are more comfortable entrusting a civil society organization with money when they see a strong board, actively involved in raising funds and ensuring accountability.

For donors and outside stakeholders, the primary role of the board is its fiduciary role, or ensuring that the finances are well cared for as legal custodian of the organization. The strength of the board, therefore, becomes a critical organizational sustainability strategy. It is unfortunate that many boards are weak and play a very minimal role in ensuring financial accountability and transparency. Many boards have been reduced to the role of check-signers only.

The transition process between the stages of development discussed above creates dynamics in an organization's governance and management. In the very early stages of the pioneer phase, there is usually what is called a management committee which combines the roles and responsibilities of the board and management. But with progress, a need becomes apparent for the separation of the management committee into a board and an executive or management team, marking the beginning of separation between management and governance roles.

Since the organization is usually still small, the pioneer leader usually organizes the first board by identifying and recruiting members. Often, the roles and responsibilities are not clear as the primary motivation for creating a board is to fulfill legal requirements. And since the director mostly recruits its members, the board is usually loyal to the leader. Once when working with a client, we observed that the director had put himself at the top of the board on the organization's organogram. While this was initially considered quite strange, it became clear that this director, perhaps out of ignorance, was just being realistic and open about what was happening, reflecting what is often the case in many organizations at this stage of development.

If the pioneer leader has managed to put up a strong management team, it is usually stronger than the board, which may actually be used to serve the interests of staff members. This is the time to recognize that NGOs are not private properties. They are public trusts. The people delegate responsibility to the board to run the trust, which in turn delegates management responsibility to the director. Therefore, it is the board and not management that is the legal custodian of the organization.

This realization has great implications on the relationship between the board and management. When an employee of one of our client organizations sued the organization for unfair dismissal, the board chair, was surprised to be served with a summons. This illustrates the degree to which the board is the legal custodian of the organization.

Though the board may initially be entirely put together by the pioneer leader, it must become self-perpetuating, meaning new members should be brought in by the board itself without undue influence. At this point, it should consolidate itself and begin to undertake its governance task as distinct from management task. While the board and management converge at the point of leadership, the governance and management tasks must be kept distinct. Failure to do this is an invitation to open conflict between the board and management.

Secretariat

If the sun says it is more powerful than the moon then let it come and shine at night

The transition from the dependent to the independent phase of organization makes the organization move from informality to formality. This usually implies the need for more specialization. While in the first phase individuals were known by their name, in the second phase they are known by their roles. Coming up with an effective structure to suit the type and work of the organization is not easy for many organizations. We have worked with organizations that took structures from larger and more complicated organizations and adopted them wholesale. Form must follow function. Organizations must first know what they will do before they share the work. When the process is reversed, conflict is inevitable because there will be people who do too much while others do nothing. It is mostly those doing nothing that encroach upon the roles of those doing too much so that they can justify remaining on the payroll.

Other organizations have managed to develop effective structures but somehow the roles and responsibilities given to individuals are not respected. Individuals are not allowed to exercise discretion and take responsibility for the outcomes of activities. Leaders interfere.

Sometimes other individuals within the organization with other sources of power interfere. An individual may bring a plan to his or her supervisor who will shoot it down. The individual may know that an idea will not work but the supervisor will still push it anyway. Roles must be respected and individuals, especially professionals, must be judged on the results they produce and given as much freedom as possible to use their own methods.

A major challenge for many organizations, especially NGOs, is the limited career progression. Many professional staff complain that if they are progress oriented, they hit the ceiling too soon. This explains why in many NGOs the space in the organization becomes too small when the staff has been trained and has gathered experience. The natural tendency of staff with experience is to try to expand his or her space. This process usually leads to conflict with the established powers in the organization. In such situations, most professional staff prefer leaving the organization altogether than deal with this conflict. This is one of the explanations for staff turnover in NGOs and other organizations. As a result, many believe that the solution is to limit training. Many NGOs no longer send staff to long-term academic courses for fear they will run away. Or may keep the staff member under bond when they do return, which may keep people in the organization who no longer want to be there.

The solution is not to stop training or putting people under a bond but to find out how to make the work of those individuals more meaningful. Leadership must find what gives meaning to these individuals and provide it. How can they make the roles they play more meaningful with their enhanced knowledge. While it may be argued that money is a major motivational factor, there are many other non-monetary factors individuals are looking for, such as recognition, involvement in decision-making and autonomy. By using the potential within individuals, it is possible to raise more money and therefore be able to pay them more.

Chapter Six	Chiku Malunga
	Organizational Wisdom in 100 African Proverbs (An Introduction to Organizational Paremiology)
	London & Abuja, Adonis & Abbey Publishers

Characteristics of an Effective Organizational Structure

Management and leadership writers who may not necessarily be organization development writers often make the assumption that all organizations must be flat organizations. While the 'flat organization' may be the ideal that all organizations must strive towards, suggesting that all organizations must be flat organizations may be misleading as different organizations may be at different stages of difference and therefore they have different structure requirements suiting their particular contexts.

An Effective Organizational a Structure is one that Ensures:

Big Picture Consciousness: Clarifies how each position relates to the whole organization and how efforts at each position contribute to the overall performance of the whole organization. Encourages self-control and self-motivation of individuals by maximizing decision-making at each level; is consistent with the vision and strategy of the organization and facilitates the achievement of results that realize the vision.

Simplicity: An organization's relative degree of bureaucracy; ability to achieve unity of command and unity of effort across the instruments of roles, responsibilities and authority. Clarifies roles and responsibilities of each position and how these relate to one another. The structure allows information and communication to flow freely. The individuals and groups know where to go for what they need, be it information, resources, or decisions.

Responsiveness: An organization's ability to quickly integrate into operational planning efforts, whether it will involve contingency or non-contingency plans; ability to quickly and adequately adjust to changes. Enables organisational stability while also allowing for flexibility to adapt to changing conditions, then enabling the organization to self-perpetuate and renew itself.

Flexibility: An organization's adaptability to task environment variables such as, political conditions, cultural issues, and coordinated partner or stakeholder involvement. The structure is consistent with the stage of development of the organization.

Sustainability: An organization's demand for resources such as manning requirements, facilities, and funding to ensure self-sustained development.

Efficiency: Level of success achieved in each of the identified essential tasks. It enables effective allocation and application of resources. It minimizes the number of people needed to do the work to ensure efficient use of resources.

Conclusion

Two rooster do not crow in the same pen
A camel is horse created by a committee

In order to strengthen relationships and minimize destructive conflict in an organization, it is important to have an effective organisational structure. Structure must evolve naturally in response to the organization's strategy or strategic plan. Forced structures feel unnatural. *A camel is a horse created by a committee.* An effective organizational structure will make the proverb; *many hands make work lighter*, a true experience in the organization.

Organizational Structure

1. What does the following proverb teach us about the importance of an effective structure in the organization?

Many hands make work lighter

2. What do the following proverbs say about the relevance of our organizational structure to the stage of our organization's development?

Organizational Structure

Many hands make work lighter
There are no short cuts to the top of a palm tree
A journey of a thousand miles started with one step

3. How do the following proverbs describe the constraints of legal requirements and stakeholder expectations on our organization's structure?

The turtle would like to dance, but just doesn't have the legs
All the stars shine but some shine brighter than others
A camel is a horse created by a committee
When the beat of the drum changes so must the step of the dance

4. How do the following proverbs describe how individuals, departments and teams are playing their roles and responsibilities in the organization?

Two fingers cannot enter into one nostril
Every man is a king in his house
A cat in its house has the teeth of a lion
Two cocks do not crow in the same pen

5. How do the following proverbs describe the relationship between leaders and subordinates as they do their work in the organization?

If the sun says it is more powerful than the moon, then let it come and shine at night

6. How does the following proverb discuss how well the board is playing its role?

When kings lose direction they become servants

Chapter Six | Chiku Malunga
Organizational Wisdom in 100 African Proverbs (An Introduction to Organizational Paremiology)
London & Abuja, Adonis & Abbey Publishers

CHAPTER SEVEN

Organizational Policies, Systems and Procedures

Rules are stronger than individual power
Life is in community
When the dog was told that there was enough meat for everyone at the feast he replied, "we will check that out at the ground level".

Introduction

All living organisms have systems or support systems that make life possible. Animals have a digestive system, a reproductive system, a urinary system and others for example. It is these systems that enable life to flow through and among the organisms. Any blockage to any system undermines the health of the organism and may sometimes result into the death of the organism. Life would cease on earth if the reproductive system was blocked. Organizations as living organisms also need healthy and functional systems to enable organizational life to flow without blockage.

When organizations grow from pioneer to independent stages, the power to run the organization must shift from individuals or the founders to the organisational policies, systems and procedures. In the independent stage of organisational development, *rules are stronger than individual power*. Problems happen when leaders and individuals resist the formulation of and adherence to appropriate policies, systems and procedures. Just as the suspicion of the dog in the proverb above, the available policies may promise so much and deliver so little.

A local non-profit organization called us to "review their policies, systems and procedures". This particular organization, when they recognized the need for policies, systems and procedures, went to a large international nongovernmental organization. They got that organization's policies, systems and procedures and literally retyped them replacing the name of that organization with their own. They said the problem was that when they tried to use the adopted policies, systems and procedures, it was like "walking in somebody else's shoes". They did not fit very well. It was this that motivated them to call for help. This is not an isolated case among many organizations especially small ones. The key lesson is *a borrowed hoe does not plough*. This chapter therefore will give a brief discussion of the major policies, systems and procedures needed in an organization and what determines what policies an organization needs. For the purpose of this book, the following definitions will be used:

- *Policy*- An agreed set of principles and guidelines for key areas of activity. A policy therefore is a statement of intent;
- *Procedure*- A set of steps for implementing the policy. They are guidelines on how the policies will be implemented in the organization;
- *Systems*- Processes guiding the use of policies and implementation of their procedures or the mechanism to hold the policies and procedures and ensuring they are internalized.

Organizational performance depends among other things on its policies, systems and procedures and how well they facilitate its work. Policies, systems and procedures play key roles in the organization, among them being: keeping the organization legal; making decision making easier and increasingly more participatory; setting standards of work and performance for staff; ensuring fairness across the whole organization; and ensuring organisational continuity by providing guidance to the people who will join the organization in the future when the current people have left.

The ultimate aim of policies, systems and procedures in an organization must be to maximize its contact with the people it serves and to encourage organisational reflection and learning. This is possible if the policies facilitate harmony and fairness among the people in the organization and with the people the organization serves as *life is in community.*

Each and every organization has its own policies, systems and procedures. The difference among organizations is that these may be: not documented or that they may not exist in written form, documented but not used, documented but used only to control and punish staff, used but with double standards i.e. the policies, systems and procedures may apply only to some but not all the members, professional staff, or documented and used to facilitate rather than hinder organisational work.

From our practice we have observed that many organizations use policies, systems and procedures selectively. They only use those policies they like. They look at policies as 'a constraint to freedom'. Policies, systems and procedures however are meant to protect the people in the organization and enhance the organizations and its people's credibility.

Using One's Best Judgment When there are No Policies

When you see a rat running into the fire, you must know that what it is running away from is hotter than the fire

Existing policies may not suffice for all situations that may arise in the organization. Dilemmas are bound to happen. Sometimes we will find ourselves in a situation where we find it difficult to make the 'right decision'. We find ourselves between 'a rock and a hard place' because there is no adequate guidance from our policies.

We may be faced with a decision to retrench staff or close the organization with no policy to guide us. Deciding to do nothing in such a situation does not help anything. We may not like both scenarios but we must act. We must choose the colder fire of the two and run into it. We may not like the fact that we will get burnt but at least we have made a rational decision under the circumstances.

Such situations however must be avoided as much as possible through anticipative policies. It is also important to note that policies, systems and procedures should be developed slowly as and when they are needed because *you cannot take a mountain by force. You must climb it slowly.* Adaptability is better than exertion.

The Evolution of Policies in an Organization

A chief must not make a new law when he or she is angry
The rod for whipping an adult should not be the same as the rod for whipping a child

Effective policies stem from a real need for them. There must be a need especially from the staff or volunteers to justify proposed policy. An organization's policies, systems and procedures originate from different factors and situations throughout an organization's life cycle. Some of these are:

1. *Stage of Development*: As a young organization grows beyond the informal stage to one with more people and complexity, it requires policies to solve problems and ensure fairness. The challenge here is to introduce formal systems which usually will incite resistance if they are seen to infringe on the benefits of informality of the first stage of organisational development. In large, complex organizations, formal systems become indispensable. The challenge there is to ensure they are helping rather than hindering work.
2. *Experience*: A particular experience not encountered before often indicates a need for a policy. For example, a staff member may suddenly die or create a conflict of interest by starting to work part-time for another organization. The organization must know how to respond. If there is no policy to deal with such cases, this is the time to introduce one. *Because she had never been burnt so the child ran into the fire.* Policies are usually formulated after an organization has undergone some difficult experience.
3. *External Forces*: Emerging issues in the external environment, like AIDS or globalization, force an organization to work and respond in new ways. Policies in gender mainstreaming and HIV and

AIDS mainstreaming are some examples of such policies. *Rather than (Check correctinon here pls) resembling one's father, resembling the* times is better. One must give up old ways to cope up with the new.

Types of Policies, Systems and Procedures

There can be no village without rules

There are many ways of categorizing policies, systems and procedures in an organization. We offer one way.

Policies

As described above, a policy is a set of principles that guide activities in an organization. A policy, therefore, is a statement of intent. In most organizations, there are four main policy areas. These are:

Monitoring and Evaluation

The monitoring and evaluation policy states how the organization intends to check progress or lack of it on its work or business at the levels of: Activities; Strategies; Goals; Mission; and Vision. Its aim is to ensure that we are on course. We are going to the right destination and that we are on the right track. *What is the point of running so fast when you are on the wrong road?*

Personnel

The personnel policy concerns itself with the welfare of people in the organization, their selection, recruitment, orientation, utilization, staff development, motivation and departure. Together these comprise a legal document called "conditions of service". The aim is to ensure that the organization becomes a living community as *life is in community*.

Administration

The administrative policy concerns itself with the efficient use of physical resources and assets in the organization. It states how the organization intends to maximize efficiency by looking at purchasing, use, management, maintenance and disposal of resources. Where there is no law, there is confusion.

Finance

The financial policy concerns itself with how the organisation intends to source and use its finances. It focuses on budgeting, accessing, allocating, managing, expanding, balancing and auditing financial resources.

Procedures

Procedures are the guidelines on how the policies will be implemented in the organisation. There are three main areas that need clear procedures. These are:

Decision-making

Procedures under decision-making clarify: the people or units that take which decisions and how; how these decisions relate to the decision taken by others; the form of responsibility that goes with the decision; who has authority for what. They also clarify: when decisions can be made and when they can be referred; how decisions are made– whether they are made by one person, through consultation, by group consensus or by majority vote; the amount of preparation that goes into decision making, the amount of information needed before a decision can be made and the amount of time needed before a decision can be made; and the way the results of the decisions are evaluated.

Accountability

Procedures under accountability clarify: who is accountable to whom; the way this accountability is put into practice; whether the organization has a hierarchy or it is a 'flat' organization in which everyone is accountable to only one person; and the consequences for not being accountable.

Communication

Procedures under communication clarify: the recognized lines of communication between individuals and units; the kind of information to be communicated; the form which such communication should take; the kind of information to be duplicated and stored. They also clarify the kind of information to be widely disseminated; the kind of information to be limited to which parties; and if there is any confidential information and how it should be treated.

Systems

Systems explain the policies and give guidelines on the principles underlying the policies. Each policy area has some systems. Some of these are:

Monitoring and Evaluation Systems

What is the point of running so fast when you are on the wrong road?

This system enables the organization to keep on course. By comparing results achieved against established targets and indicators, staffs know how close or far away they are drifting from their original course. Therefore, effective monitoring and evaluation tools are critical.

The uses of Monitoring and Evaluation are: strategic planning, program Improvement, performance accounting, and performance forecasting; early warning, program implementation and program accountability; benchmarking and quality management.

Monitoring and evaluation are two sides of the same coin, differing only in their frequency and range of decision-making. Monitoring means observing and collecting information to see trends and directions that validate that the program is still on course or if a change is necessary. Evaluation is the comprehensive analysis of the operation over time to support strategy and planning. Evaluation is a less frequent form of monitoring. It is deeper and leads to more fundamental decisions.

To be effective, monitoring and evaluation must be logical, focused systematic and conscious. Monitoring and evaluation are continuous processes that go through the following stages: establishing benchmark/baseline information to get a clear picture on the current reality; planning to make decisions and establish priorities of the program or project; setting goals and objectives to define the desired future to result from the work of the project or program; establishing indicators or measures of progress; collecting data using tools based on indicators; and analyzing data to check progress and formulate learning for improvement;

Reflection and Learning System

The people who cannot kindle their own fire are easy to defeat
Knowledge is like a baobab tree, no one person can embrace it alone

In many African villages, elders literally lit a fire in the evenings to informally discuss challenges and opportunities facing the village and how to address the challenges and make use of the opportunities. Those villages that did not do this could easily be defeated by natural and human enemies. At family level, it was the role of grandparents to tell folk tales to grand children around a fire. The aim was entertainment but much more importantly it was teaching the children and entrenching in them cultural values and identity. Those children that missed this type of education did not have enough cultural and social foundation and could easily be defeated. On the night after the wedding, the couple was not allowed to immediately go for a honey moon. The first night, the elders from both the man's and the woman's side lit a fire in the house of the newly married couple and talked with the newly married couple late into the night about marriage and family values and practices. Marriages that missed that type of fire lacked a strong foundation.

Organizations too must light a fire around which organisational members can talk and draw lessons for improving practice or they will be easily defeated from within or from without. Organizations must set up reflection and learning systems that must enable them to decipher what is in people's heads, put them on the table, and together create a common understanding of what the organization is and what it should be and how to get there. Without this type of talking, we assume that we are altogether when in reality we are not. After working for over seven months as a consultant on a major change program in an organization, I was surprised to be asked by one of the directors why the organization was going through the change process.

While the purpose of monitoring and evaluation is to track progress in the implementation of the project activities, the purpose of the reflection and learning system is to draw lessons for improving implementation and practice. In terms of learning from failure for example, the system helps the organization *not to look at where it fell but where it tripped*. It may take place as a retreat that takes place towards the end of the year and may be attended by members of the board, management and staff representatives including some external stakeholders for objectivity and independence. Using an external facilitator role, the organization reflects on where it stands in relation to where it wants to go. Conscious organizational learning enables the organization to continually challenge itself and raise its bar. In setting up organisational learning systems, it is important to remember that *knowledge is like a baobab tree, no one person can embrace it alone.* In other words, everyone's knowledge in the organization counts. We normally think that the people at the top know or only a few people have knowledge. But for organisational learning systems to be effective, everyone's knowledge must be sought, respected and utilized.

Chapter Seven | Chiku Malunga
Organizational Wisdom in 100 African Proverbs (An Introduction to Organizational Paremiology)
London & Abuja, Adonis & Abbey Publishers

The first step is to reflect on the organization's ideal picture and then to reflect on how the organization's practice in the year has helped to move the organization towards the ideal picture or not.

The process is guided by the action learning cycle questions: what is the ideal picture of our organization? What did we say we would accomplish this year in order to move towards this ideal picture? From our plans, what have we achieved and what have we not achieved? (Each department and unit presents its annual report)? What has helped us to move towards our ideal picture and what has hindered us? What lessons/insights can we draw from the successes and helping factors; the failures and hindering factors? And how can we use the lessons in our plans for next year so that we can build on our strengths and helping factors and eliminate our failures and hindering factors?

In addition to drawing lessons from program implementation, the annual participatory reviews offer opportunity for the organization to assess its internal capacity to effectively carry out in projects and programs. The following rated tool can help in organizational self–assessments at the annual participatory review:

Organizational Self-assessment Tool   Rate 0 – 5   0 = non-existent 5 = excellent

Element	Rate 0 - 5	Explanation
1. Clarity of organizational vision, direction and focus		
2. Clarity of organizational identity		
3. Clarity of organizational image among stakeholders		
4. Clarity of and adherence to organizational values		
5. Clarity of organizational structure: roles and responsibilities of departments and individuals		
6. Relationship and communication		

between international, regional, national and area offices		
1. Policies, systems and procedures: • Financial management • Grants management • Human Resources • Conditions of service • Administration • Monitoring and evaluation • Gender mainstreaming • HIV and AIDS mainstreaming		
8. Skills and competencies to much our work		
9. Adequacy of financial and material resources against our target		
10. Networking and collaboration		
11. General level of effectiveness of our programs		

In order to preserve the learning and build organizational memory the insights must be documented, published and disseminated to both internal and external stakeholders. Many organizations write annual reports on activity achievements and failures. While this is very important, it is even more important to write a separate annual report on lessons and insights gained in the year. The programs department may write the activity accomplishments report while the capacity building department may write the lessons and insights report.

At the end of a period of time, like five years of the country strategic paper, it may be possible to write an 'organisational lessons book' or document on best practices.

Operational System

When Action Speaks Words become Silent

The operational system shows how the organization has organized its strategy and the different elements that need to be integrated and managed. It clarifies how different projects link together or how the organization tends to handle them if they do not. It also shows how people on different projects should relate to one another to ensure synergy. This system challenges the organization to focus on the appropriateness of its strategies. Combined with monitoring and evaluation, this system shows whether the strategy is a success or a failure.

Specifically, the system may look at: the amount of detail required before implementing a project, what needs to be in written form and what does not. It may also look at flow charts or Pert diagrams including how objectives will be measured, by whom and to whom reporting will be done and the type of resources– human, material etc are required. The organization may also decide to start off with less detailed planning and work things throughout the life of the project.

Personnel System

People are More Important than Things:

- Human Resources Development-The human resources development system ensures that the people in the organization are competent enough and motivated enough to do their jobs effectively. The development of individuals and teams in the organization may happen through a number of ways. Some of these are: assessment of competencies, training individuals, coaching and developmental counselling, mentoring and many others. In most organizations, the development of individuals and teams is the most neglected part of organisational life. Organizations must ensure that development of human resources go beyond mere training to include personal mastery in which individuals take responsibility of their own self-development and consciously link their development to that of the organization. Human resources development must not be limited to members of staff only. Board members and volunteers must also be included.

- Conditions of Service- This is the system that holds together all the rules and regulations that govern how the individuals and groups will work. This system specifies organisational policies, career paths, gender relations, grievance procedures, disciplinary codes; and relevant personal information.
- Recruitment and Selection- Most 'people' problems in organizations could be prevented if the people were carefully selected and recruited in the first place. Wrong people in wrong jobs cause friction, which drains the organization's energy. In recruiting people, ways of understanding prospective employees' values and how these would fit with the organization's values must be given more emphasis than basing recruitment decisions on impressive CVs alone.
- Job Designs and Descriptions- It is important to clearly clarify what the job is about, how it fits into the overall mission of the organization and what is expected of the individual. It is also very necessary to clarify the resources and support system available to enable them to do their work. The job design and description must specify the expected results while leaving room on the methods the individual or team may wish to employ. Board members and volunteers too need clear job designs and descriptions.
- Remuneration- The remuneration system focuses on the salary structure and the appraisal procedures. This is one of the most critical systems for any organization. Organizations that have competitive salaries will attract and retain better people than those, which do not. The remuneration system, however, must look beyond money alone. It must also look into such non-monetary issues as recognition, responsibility, self-development etc. The organization must also reward teamwork and team spirit.

- Administration- The administrative system is concerned with the proper usage of the organization's assets. It looks at the organization's filing (storage and retrieval of information), use of equipment, procurement and supply, logistical support etc. It focuses on preventing misuse of power and resources in the organization.
- Finance- The financial system is the most sensitive system in any organization because it is an area most people are opens to abuse and corruption. Therefore, every organization needs tight controls. The first part of the financial system is how the finances are secured. Different organizations have different ways of securing finances or resources (e.g., marketing, public relations, fundraising, etc.) This is a very important aspect of organisational life because no organization can exist without money and therefore merits due attention. Then when the money or resources have come into the organization, it must then ensure they are fairly distributed, regularly checked and properly accounted for.

Information and Communication Systems

A repeated incision shines brighter
Useful information is more important than money

All the above systems are served by the information system, which is in turn served by the communication system. The information system ensures that organisational decisions are made based on factual information rather than mere assumptions or hearsay. This system enables the organization to have an accurate, balanced and unbiased picture of what is happening both inside the organization and its task environment. Most organizations are weak on this point. The organization must carefully think through the information it needs to run smoothly. The organization formulates questions around this information that the information system must answer. This will ensure that the system focuses only on information necessary and help people avoid collecting irrelevant or unnecessary information.

The organization or rather the people in the organization must come up with tools for collecting the information, which are 'user friendly' and take as less time as possible but at the same time are exhaustive. When the information has been collected, it must be organized in a way that makes it easy to retrieve. It must also be organized in such a way that it is easy to cross check data and information over time and among the different parts of the organization. This ease of cross checking makes it possible to make decisions based on the information and the data.

In order to ensure organisational effectiveness, information must not only be collected and stored well. It must be well communicated. Lack of effective communication is a major problem in most organizations. An effective communication system must: use both formal and informal ways of communicating. Many times people are more free and real in informal settings than in formal settings. When used properly, the informal ways or channels of communication reinforce the formal channels of communication. In addition, it must ensure two ways rather than one-way communication– the system must encourage dialogue rather than 'telling'. It must encourage both the 'sender' and 'receiver' to empathize with each other and see things from 'the other's point of view'. It must also reduce lines of communication– when there are more people in the chain of communication the chances of distorting the information increases. If possible, it works better to talk directly to people than to delegate.

In more practical terms, communication in an organization could be enhanced through one-on-one meetings, effective group meetings, suggestion boxes, open door policies and anonymous surveys among others. When we have communicated effectively, gossip and hearsay will be reduced in the organization. Tension will be eased and people will make rational and informed decisions.

An effective format to use in writing a policy, its systems and procedures would include the following points:

Chapter Seven	Chiku Malunga
	Organizational Wisdom in 100 African Proverbs (An Introduction to Organizational Paremiology)
	London & Abuja, Adonis & Abbey Publishers

1. Current situation;
2. Rational for the policy at the current time (4–5 statements);
3. Purpose and working objectives;
4. Scope (Who and what areas does it cover? What are its limits?);
5. Underlying principles;
6. Shared definitions of the key words;
7. Relevant procedures;
8. Cost implications;
9. Exceptions to the policy (if any).

Policies and Values

Responsible people do not need rules

If all the people in an organization had the same values, there would be no need for policies. Trust that each person would act responsibly and rationally in the interest of the organization would suffice. Policies are needed to protect the interests of the organization. Protecting the organization and its interests depends on the congruence between the shared values of the organization and the behaviours of the people towards the organization.

Values are a person's sense of right and wrong; and what's important and what's not. Values guide a person's behaviour. Each organization must agree on what its shared values must be. Each person in the organization must commit to live by these values at least during working hours and in all matters pertaining to the organization and its image.

The foundation for effective policies, therefore, is their conscious connection to the shared values of the organization. People's values may be known by the way they react to a situation. When there is no policy and a situation occurs, like two employees start having an affair for example, leaders are often surprised to realize for the first time how different they are in the way they look at moral and ethical issues. Some may take a conservative standard like, 'fire them'. Others may take a liberal stand like, 'help the people concerned to manage their relationship without disrupting the organization and its work'. The difference in values on such matters may create destructive tension and conflict. It is these types of differences that call for the need for a set of shared values, which are translated into policy statements. In this way, policies ensure consistency and fairness in decision-making and implementation.

When diversity in values increases, there will be need for more policies. When diversity in values decrease there will be less need for more policies. The same also applies to responsibility. When people are more responsible, there will be less need for more policies. When people are less responsible, there will be more need for more policies.

As the organization moves along its stages of development, there is less need for policies in the dependent stage because the organization is built on trust in the leader and camaraderie among organizational members. The greatest diversity in values occurs as the organization moves and is in the independent stage. Understandably, this is when the organization needs the most policies. When the policies become too much, they start constraining the liberty of the organizational members. They once again see the need for depending more on values than rules. This leads to a reduction to the necessary minimum in the number of policies. This is a main characteristic of the interdependent stage of organization. The same also applies to responsibility. The crisis that ushers the organization to the independent phase often reveals that the high level of responsibility experienced in the organization was assumed rather than actual. This leads to the many policies in the independent phase. The pain coming out of the constraints imposed by the many policies motivates the people in the organization to develop their sense of responsibility. When this is matured, the organization is ready to shed off some of the constraining policies as it enters into the interdependency stage of development. In the interdependent stage, therefore, responsibility is actual rather than assumed.

The main challenge for organizations, therefore, may not be to increase the number of policies, systems and procedures but to reduce their need through building the values base of the organization and the level of responsibility among the people in the organization. In this way, self-management rather than control through rules becomes possible.

Leaders must be exemplary in living the values of the organization. They should also be exemplary in living out the policies, systems and procedures: when the chief limps all the subjects limp too.

Conclusion

If we stand tall today it is because we stand on the shoulders of those who have gone before us
It should not only be right for the goat to hit the dog and wrong for the dog to bite the goat

In summary, the following points should be observed to ensure that the organization's policies, systems and procedures are effective:

1. Values – An organization's policies must be consciously linked to its shared values. The values must form the base upon which the policies are founded.
2. Fairness– While no policy can please everyone in the organization, each policy should be aimed at being as fair as possible to as many people as possible. People should not feel that in the organization *it is right for the goats to hit the dogs but wrong for the dogs to bite the goats*. In addition to fairness, a policy must represent the interests of as many people as possible. A policy must not be self-serving to the people who formulate it, but it must primarily serve the interests of the organization. This is why in some parliaments; an amendment to the constitution is not implemented by the current parliament but the next one. This ensures that the amendment was indeed in the interest of the nation and not the members of parliament who made it.
3. In order to achieve the foregoing, it is important to involve as many individuals and groups as possible within the organization. The wider the diversity consulted in formulating the policy, the higher its chances of success. Since

constitutionally it's the board's responsibility to formulate policies, the board may want to leave the other groups out. This may lead to ineffective policies because the board is often out of tune of ground realities. It is important, therefore, that the board involves those people who will be directly affected by the policies while maintaining its responsibility for the formulation and approval of the policies.

4. A policy must be responsive. It must be responsive to the legislation requirements, task environment factors, and financial implications of the policy on political, and economic, technological and social issues. In addition to being responsive, policies must be proactive and preventive in nature. They must be formulated before they are needed rather than later.

5. Lastly, a policy must take a long-term view. It must take into consideration both current, short-term and long-term issues. A policy must not be something, which can be changed any time and anyhow though at the same time it must not be cast in stone. When conditions change, the policy must be reviewed to ensure its relevance.

Organizational Policies, Procedures and Systems:

1. What do the following proverbs say about our organizational policies?

There can be no village without rules
Rules are stronger than power

2. What do the following proverbs say about the consistency between our organizational policies and how they are used?

When the dog was told that there would be enough meat for everyone at the feast he replied, "We will check that out at the ground level".

3. What does the following proverb say about how well the organization handles issues on which there are no policies or the policies are not clear?

When you see a rat running into the fire, you must know that what it is running away from is hotter than the fire

4. What do the following proverbs say about how policies are developed in the organization?

A chief must not make a new law when he or she is angry
The rod for whipping an adult should not be the same as the rod for whipping a child

5. How does the following proverb describe the effectiveness of our organizational information and communication systems?

A repeated incision shines brighter

6. What does the following proverb say about our need for policies vis a vis responsibility?

Responsible people do not need rules

7. What do the following proverbs tell us about our organizational and reflection and learning systems?

The people who cannot kindle their own fire are easy to defeat
Knowledge is like a baobab tree no one person can embrace it alone
Do not look at where you fell, look at where you tripped

8. How do the following proverbs describe the effectiveness of our policies?

If we stand tall today it is because we stand on the shoulders of those who have gone before us

It should not only be right for the goat to hit the dog and wrong for the dog to bite the goat

CHAPTER EIGHT

Cultivating Organizational Wisdom:
The Organization Development Process

Advice is like mushrooms, the wrong kind can be fatal
To see a snail's eyes one must be patient
A fruit does not ripe in a day
A patient mouse in a young banana tree will one day eat a ripe banana

Introduction

Organizational growth and development are natural processes. They are happening by themselves without intervention all the time. Plants as biological systems have the propensity to grow towards the sun for light and to go deeper into the soil for nutrients. Living systems, including organizations, have the natural propensity to grow bigger and better. The added value that OD brings to the process is 'consciousnesses – the consciousness to create a more conducive environment for the growth and development to flourish. In achieving better organizational development and growth, consciousness precedes being which in turn precedes doing and relating.

One day, while on a consultancy assignment in the Manica province of Mozambique with a friend, Alfredo Mazive, we bought some two very big tilapia fish from the road side fish sellers because we were very hungry after a hard day's work. We were so hungry we wanted the fish to be roasted immediately. The boys took us to a nearby village canteen where we asked some women working at the canteen to roast the fish for us.

While waiting for the fish to be roasted we bought some drinks; after the drinks we began to dance to some Bob Marley music which was being played in the canteen. We danced until the tape finished. The owner put on some Botswana music. It also played until it finished. We were now getting frustrated by the delays of the women in the kitchen. Alfredo went to make an inquiry. He asked an elderly man who was the owner of the canteen. What the man said to Alfredo has stuck with me since that day. He said, "My son, if you want well roasted fish you must be patient– well roasted fish especially that which is roasted on charcoal fire, takes time. These women are very experienced women and they want you to really enjoy your fish when they bring it. Well roasted fish takes time to prepare and cook".

Thirty minutes later, true to the elderly man's words we had the best charcoal roasted fish I had ever had. We danced some more and continued our journey after giving a generous tip to the women.

A mistake many organizations make is to seek and initiate OD processes when they are already in a crisis. OD processes work better when they are done proactively. This gives the organization adequate time to go through the process sanely. They can also go through the process with patience. Life cannot be hurried. We should not wait until when we are very hungry to start seeking help. Prevention is better than cure. If we want a really good and effective OD process we must be patient. Wisdom does not come overnight. This patience, however, is not possible in a crisis situation. There are no short cuts to the top of the palm tree.

Stages of the OD Process

The success or failure of an OD process or program is often determined by how well the process is managed. There are five stages in the OD process. These are: the orientation, contracting, organizational assessment, implementation; and monitoring and evaluation phases. Being a long-term process, there are a lot of potential challenges and obstacles along the way.

This chapter will discuss the OD process and how to manage it effectively. The OD process is about an organization dealing with

---

Chapter Eight | Chiku Malunga
Organizational Wisdom in 100 African Proverbs (An Introduction to Organizational Paremiology)
London & Abuja, Adonis & Abbey Publishers

advice on how to improve its processes. Just as advice is like mushrooms and the wrong type can prove fatal, the type of advice that the organization seeks and uses in the process is of critical importance. Effective management of the OD process is the way for cultivating organizational wisdom.

The Orientation Phase

It is the sick person who calls for the doctor
The dog that barks the loudest does not bite
Bedbugs are known by the person who sleeps in the room

This phase starts with the organization or its leaders recognizing a need for external support on some issue that needs to be addressed. Only those leaders who have some awareness of what OD is may find it natural to approach an OD practitioner. Those who do not have such awareness may be at a loss at whom to approach or what to look for in a consultant. It is important that leaders know what to look for in a consultant for their organisational needs to avoid getting wrong mushrooms which may prove fatal to the organization. Impressive qualifications and CVs alone are not sufficient to ensure a consultant will be effective in a situation. Often times, those with the most impressive CVs and qualifications may not be the best thus the proverb, "the dogs that bark the loudest doest not bite".

In this phase, the client contacts the consultant with a felt need. This might be through a letter, a phone call or a visit. Sometimes it may be through an advert for bidding in a paper. The most important thing is that it must be the client needing the consultant and not vice versa. An OD practitioner can only be effective if he or she is invited and not when he or she invites themselves into the organization. The consultant's power is tied to the invitation.

This phase also involves the first meeting between the consultant and the client to 'understand' the request. Often times, what clients ask for may not be what they need. Many times what clients present as their problems may only be symptoms of real and underlying issues. This meeting also helps to know whether OD would be the most appropriate way to address the issue facing the client. After the meeting, an agreement is reached whether OD would indeed help in the situation or not. It takes a high level of maturity and professionalism on the side of the consultant to be frank with the client that OD is not what he or she is looking for if this happens to be the case. It is also important to discuss with the client on the 'depth of the intervention that the client is ready for'. Sometimes clients consciously do not want to go deep enough. This too must be respected.

Since there are different approaches that might be employed in improving organisational effectiveness, some of the signs indicating that OD would be more appropriate are:

- The same problem keeps recurring despite various efforts to arrest it;
- You know that there is a problem in the organization but you cannot quite figure out what it is;
- The organization is faced with dilemmas too difficult to resolve;
- The organization is contemplating or has experienced major changes (e.g. change in size, focus, identity, strategy and projects);
- There is confusion about identity, roles and responsibilities;
- There are high levels of staff turnover and frustration;
- There are relationship problems; individuals, departments, board and staff 'do not see eye to eye'; there are high levels of suspicion and lack of trust; people are happier outside the organization than inside;
- Different departments or projects become too autonomous creating co-ordination problems;
- There is a general lack of commitment to the organization and its goals;
- People feel powerless and energy is spent on pointing fingers at each other rather than addressing problems.

After agreeing that the situation would indeed be addressed through OD, the consultant *'listens with two ears'* to what the client is asking for and how they feel about what they are asking for. It is important on the outset to gauge the amount of 'energy' in the organization to address what they are asking for. It is important, therefore, to establish whether it is their problem or somebody else is telling them that they need to address this. In many non-profit organizations for example, requests that come to the OD consultant are in reality a donor's and not the organization's request. In such situations, the consultant must explain to the client what OD is and what going through an OD process would mean for the client. The consultant must bring home the importance of commitment and ownership to the process on the part of the client if it is to be a success.

It is also important for the client to concretize the above explanations through sharing with the client in his or her experiences. He or she must explain what he or she has observed and learned in working with other organizations in similar situations. The most important thing to explain is that as a process consultant, he or she works with the client and not for the client or to the client. While the consultant will do his or her best, 'working with the client' leaves the responsibility of the success and failure of the OD process with the client.

The Contracting Phase

Birds agree first before they fly together

Before the actual work starts it is important to formalize the relationship between the consultant and the organization. The contract protects both the organization and the consultant by clarifying what is expected of each party. A contract must specify: expected outputs by the consultant, the role the client will play in supporting the consultant, reporting procedures, how costs will be met; amount of fees to be paid to the consultant and how payment will be made and termination procedures of the contract.

A clarification from these points helps to address some of the potential challenges inherent in the OD process. Some of these challenges are:

Ethical issues– one of the key ethical issues facing many consultants working in situations similar to where we are working is the issue of giving the client 'gifts'. Some clients will 'expect' and sometimes demand the consultant to give them a 'commission' for offering them a contract. This is a very difficult ethical issue in a culture where this is a norm. OD being a profession founded on strong values and ethics, it is important for each consultant to make an ethical stand in their practice and stick with it. We have observed that this issue is relatively more critical among 'beginning' and freelance consultants. Experienced consultants can use their experience and the professional identity they have built during their years of practice to 'frighten off' 'commission seekers'. Consultants operating from an organization can hide behind their 'organisational policies, systems and procedures', which 'do not allow us to do such a thing'. We have found building one's identity through enhancing competence and character to be a main strategy to avoiding being caught up in such unethical behaviour. Another way is to have a good hospitality strategy. When clients visit the consultants' organization, it is important to 'treat them well'. This could be through a lunch, a night out or any other legitimate and ethical entertainment. Cultivating an ethical relationship based on mutual respect and trust makes it difficult for the client to demand what he or she may now know is not part of your values and principles. Through such practice reputation for integrity may spread from actual to potential clients through word of mouth. We have also found 'striving to be the best in the field' or creating a reputation for being the best and, therefore, making oneself 'indispensable' to be the most effective antidote to having to use or being forced to use bribes.

Some of the unethical issues might include misrepresenting one's qualifications and experience as a consultant, agreeing to undertake an intervention in which one has no skill, experience or competence, colluding with particular groups in the organization to 'attack' the other groups or individuals, forcing the client to go the way of the consultant rather than the way the client's wants.

Sustaining interest– many organizations have become accustomed to their chronic problems and they do not care to address them. Many times they will only call for an external consultant because of an acute problem. They will call for a consultant because they are experiencing serious pain. Pain, however, is only meant to be a motivator for calling for an OD intervention because OD is primarily aimed at addressing the chronic rather than the acute problems. What happens most of the times is that when the pain goes away with the first among the many recommended interventions, the client's interest often wanes. Sustaining the client's interest throughout the process is quite a big challenge. This is why in the contract the client must commit to a long-term process. It may be important to involve the donor sponsoring the process to commit to fund the process rather than a single intervention if need be. Sometimes it may be important to refuse signing the contract if the client only wants to 'use' the consultant on a one-off event, as a means to getting funding only as an example.

Belief in foreign consultants– many organizations in developing countries still believe that a consultant must come from America or Europe or at least from outside the country. This is shown through recruitment and remuneration procedures of consultants, which favour consultants from these areas. Where there is an obvious lack of competent local consultants, it is justifiable to import consultants from outside. It only becomes an issue when American or European consultants are preferred simply because they are from the America or Europe. Competent local consultants have more advantages than imported consultants primarily because they understand their situation better. Combined teams of local and imported consults may also be appropriate where local and international perspectives are needed. All in all, most organizations have a challenge to overcome the problem of 'too much belief in imported consultants'. At the same time, local consultants need to understand that respect and acceptance are not given on a silver platter; they have to be earned through excellent practice.

Over-dependence on the Consultant by the Client– As the OD process is progressing; the client may develop more and more dependence on the consultant. The consultant may also want to prolong the relationship more than is necessary for other reasons such as financial gain. Clarification on this matter in the contract helps avoid such situations from arising. This is why the contract must specify the duration of the relationship and clear roles and responsibilities of the client and the consultant. Adherence to these enables the consultant to maintain a healthy social and professional distance from the client. This helps the client to avoid being 'swallowed up' by the culture of the organization. It is important for clients to always remember that the aim of OD is to create increasingly self-reliant organizations, which are more and more capable of solving their own problems and addressing their challenges.

Attention to Impact or Capacity Dilemma– Donors' and stakeholders' requirement for organizations to demonstrate impact makes it difficult for the organizations to give enough attention to building their internal capacity. Project activities, writing project and financial reports and deadlines take most of the time leaving none for internal capacity building. Many OD processes are frustrated as 'new projects and activities' suddenly become priorities pushing the OD process into the background. It is important before signing the contract to explain to the client the time demands of the OD process and obtain a commitment that this time will be made available. This must be reflected in the contract.

In order to ensure that the OD process will be a success, it is important at the contracting phase to choose a 'change group' in the organization. This group must be made up of people who can influence others in the organization. It is this group that will be the primary interface between the consultant and the organization during the OD process. The consultant discusses the OD process plan with this group and encourages them to discuss the plan among themselves. The 'change group' is a learning opportunity about leadership and development among the people involved. The consultant is part of this group and he or she eventually withdraws as the OD process is nearing the end. The concept of the 'change group' is a sustainability strategy as it ensures the continuation of the OD process and benefits after the contract with the client has expired.

Organizational Assessment Phase

A healthy chick comes from a healthy egg

The first activity in the OD program is conducting an assessment. An assessment stems from two main needs. These are: to know the current health status of the organization and to know the effects of the interventions and take corrective measures as a result.

Assessments must be focused on the whole organization or on the aspect of the organization affected by the issue at hand. Even when the assessment focuses on an aspect of the organization, it is important to undertake it in the perspective of the whole organization. This enables the client to see how efforts in this particular aspect are contributing to the overall organisational effectiveness.

To be effective, assessments must be solution rather than problem centered. It is often more effective to ask people what they want first rather than what their problems are. The development model presented in chapter 1 begins with the creation of an ideal picture of the desired situation. The assessment process is therefore based on, "what can help us or hinder us from realizing the ideal picture or the desired situation?"

Data analysis follows data collection. This is usually done in a feedback workshop. Joint data analysis with the client is encouraged for a number of reasons. Among these are: it reinforces ownership to the process, it helps clarify and separate perceptions from real issues and it helps in joint prioritization and action planning.

Part of the data analysis process involves challenging the client to see the contradictions in their behaviors and therefore how their decisions and actions have created the current undesired situation. By seeing how responsible they were in creating the current undesired situation, they are also encouraged to see how responsible they are in creating the desired situation.

To be effective, the assessments must: assess potential for action in the client (readiness, time, resources), help people see the 'whole picture' and the relationships within the picture, focus on the desired future and not to be caught up in the negative past or present and recommend interventions and tasks that people can do for themselves

The output of an assessment is a participatorily agreed prioritized capacity building plan. An example of such a plan is given below for an imaginary organization called Human Rights Centre (HRC):

HRC's INTERNAL CAPACITY BUILDING ISSUES			
1. Inadequate financial sustainability	HRC has a diversified and sustainable financial and material resources	Expand the financial and material resource base of HRC	• Identify alternative sources of funding • Write proposals • Identify fund raising strategies • Implement realistic and cost effective fund raising strategies
2. Number of staff and volunteers versus area of coverage at secretariat and district levels	HRC's activities are focused and concentrated	Balance number of staff and volunteers with area of coverage	• Review effectiveness of activities in current areas of work • Review adequacy of staff and volunteers working in the areas • Determine areas to work in • Strengthen and develop current staff and volunteers • Recruit additional staff and volunteers
3. Ineffective policies, systems and procedures	HRC has effective policies, systems and procedures in the areas of • Administration • Financial Management • Human Resource (Including Conditions of Service, staff and volunteer protection, Gender and HIV/AIDS mainstreaming)	Develop appropriate policies, systems and procedures	• Review existing policies, systems and procedures • Implement new policies, systems and procedures • Monitor and evaluate effectiveness
4. Inadequate skills and competencies to match the scope of work	HRC has adequate and relevant skills for their scope of work	Develop a staff, board and volunteer development plan	• Conduct skills and competencies assessment against the newly agreed programmes and

Chapter Eight | Chiku Malunga
Organizational Wisdom in 100 African Proverbs (An Introduction to Organizational Paremiology)
London & Abuja, Adonis & Abbey Publishers

			activities
			• Train and develop current personnel
			• Recruit needed personnel
			• Orient existing and new personnel to the scope of work
			• Conduct exchange study programmes locally and internationally
			• Develop and implement a staff, board and volunteer appraisal system
5. Need for a more appropriate and effective structure	HRC has a facilitative structure	Develop an appropriate structure for HRC	• Review current structure
			• Develop a new structure
			• Implement the new structure
			Monitor and evaluate the new structure

For implementation, the plan must show the time frame, the individuals responsible for the activities and indicators that will show whether the activity has been successful or not. This brings us to the next phase, which is:

The Implementation Phase

It is not by just looking at a newly married wife that she will become pregnant

As stated elsewhere, we have observed non-implementation of capacity building plans to be a major challenge in the OD process. The most beautiful and well-constructed capacity building plan will mean nothing if people in the organization do not work to implement it. The commitment of the organization to its own improvement will be known by its commitment to implement the capacity building plan. In order to help the organization implement its capacity building plan and conquer inertia the following suggestions might help:

Ensure the first intervention is successful – When people are successful the first time, they develop faith to do more in order to create more success. In prioritizing the interventions therefore, it is important to start with those interventions with the highest chance of success. It is also important to start with the easiest and least sensitive interventions. This helps to reduce fear, which is inherent in most change processes. We have observed fear to be a great hindrance among organisational leaders to adopting OD interventions. It is important, therefore, to be sensitive to this fact.

Give enough authority to the change group– to ensure that the interventions are implemented and followed through, it is important that the leadership in the organization must give adequate authority and responsibility to the change group and not meddle. It then becomes the responsibility of this group to see to it that the capacity building plan is being followed and that the organization is creating the required time and space for the implementation of the capacity building plan. Individual leaders may be 'too busy' to manage the implementation of the capacity building plan. At the same time, giving the responsibility of managing the capacity building plan to the change group offers them a chance to learn and practice leadership skills. In order to ensure that more people benefit, it may be necessary to let people join and leave the change group after some time.

Allocate enough resources to the process– In order to ensure effective implementation, ensure there are adequate financial and material resources for the process. It is frustrating to get people excited and committed to the process only to end at an anticlimax because there are no resources to continue the process. In our practice, we have observed this to be a major challenge undermining OD programs. At CADECO, we have sometimes waited for two years before an organisational capacity building plan can be implemented because there were no financial resources to back the plan. This is why during the orientation and contracting phase it is important to discuss in detail the financial and material resource implications of the OD process. It may be important to delay starting an OD process and help the organization find adequate resources before engaging in the process. The organization must also be willing to deploy its best people to manage the process. The quality of the people on the change team will determine the success or failure of the process.

Involve all People– In order to be a success, the OD process must gain an organisation wide acceptance and commitment. It is therefore important to provide as much information as possible on the aims and activities of the process. It is also important to communicate to the people the successes and achievements of the process. It is also important to celebrate the small successes and achievements. As many people as possible must be involved as much as possible. People will only commit when they feel that they are part and parcel of the change process and that it is in their interest. People will only commit if they are adequately involved.

Don't rush– The time schedules of the capacity building plans must be realistic. It is important to recognize the fact that organizations exist to fulfill their missions by implementing projects in their task environments. They do not exist to build their internal capacity. It is also important to recognize that the success of an organization is not normally measured by how well 'internally capacitated' it is but by its performance in the task environment. For these reasons, it is important to be realistic with time allocations to the capacity building plans. When we were just beginning our OD practice, we used to cram an organization with OD interventions in a year. We have come to realize that it may take anything between 12 to 24 months and sometimes more to effectively implement an organization's capacity building plan. This gives adequate time to the organization to practice what they have learned in the interventions before going to the next intervention. This strengthens the learning spirit, which is crucial to the success of the OD process.

The Monitoring and Evaluation Phase

The person who does not know where he is going will not realize it when he has arrived
What is the point of running so fast when you are on the wrong road?

Undoubtedly, one of the most challenging issues in managing the OD process is 'how to measure progresses. It is relatively easier to measure progress in 'project implementation' as compared to the intangible issues of organizational capacity. It is this lack of clarity on how to measure organizational capacity that sometimes makes it difficult for organizations to convince donors to sponsor their organizational capacity building initiatives. This is because donors want 'hard evidence' that their money is making impact in the organization's task environment.

It is important however to note that an organization's ultimate measure of its capacity is its performance at all levels. These are: efficiency as a measure of activities, effectiveness as a measure of strategies, impact as a measure of goals, legacy as a measure of the mission and; societal transformation as a measure of the vision. The basis of the foregoing reasoning is that only an organization with capacity can produce results in the task environment. One observes that as one move from efficiency to societal transformation, the organization needs more and more capacity. One also observes that as one moves from efficiency to societal transformation, it becomes more and more difficult to objectively and quantitatively measure progress. It becomes more and more difficult to have clear indicators of progress. This difficulty creates the need for specific indicators of organizational capacity. This makes it possible to measure progress of organizational capacity apart from the results the organization is producing.

Measuring organizational capacity on its own apart from the results the organization is producing makes it possible to show the link between the organization's capacity and its results. This is necessary for organizational leaders and stakeholders to appreciate the importance of organizational capacity building. Through this, it is possible to show that those organizations that have 'more capacity' have also better results in their task environments.

Indicators of organizational capacity are based on the organizational assessment tools used in the organization. Since the assessment measures 'what is the situation?' in the organization, the monitoring and evaluation system measures 'how the situation is changing' using the same assessment factors. The table below illustrates the point:

Table Monitoring and Evaluating an OD Process
Rating 0 – 5, 0 = Nonexistent   5 = Excellent

Component	Assessment Rating	Assessment during or after OD Process	Percentage Change
1. Financial and material resources			
2. Skills and competencies in the organization			
3. Policies, systems and procedures			
4. Structure			
5. Roles and responsibilities			
6. Strategy			
7. Vision and			

mission			
8. Culture and values			
9. Governance, leadership and management			
10. External relationships			

The organization must through consensus or otherwise rate these components during the assessment phase. After agreeing, the people must give the reasons for the agreed rate. The organization must put in place a monitoring system that will enable it to notice changes on the assessment ratings as the OD process is progressing. At the end of the OD process the organization must also 'measure' the percentage changes from the assessment measures by consensus or otherwise. The people must also give reasons for the new rating. The rates enable the consultant and the client to come up with themes, which point out to the issues needing attention and also an indication over time on how these issues are being resolved.

We have found the above tool to be useful in measuring objectively and 'quantitatively' changes resulting from an OD process. Its major weakness however may be that people in the organization may mistake having the 'component' like strategy or a mission statement or policies which were not there before the OD process for having built the organization's capacity. The point to emphasize is that it is not having these components that signify capacity but the benefits that flow from an effective use of these components. For this reason, we have found complementing the above tool with the one below as being more effective in measuring and monitoring organisational capacity.

Table OD Processes Monitoring and Evaluation Tool
Rating 0 = Extremely Poor, 3 = Good 5 = Exceptionally Good

Organisational process	Assessment Rating	Rating During or after OD Process	Percentage Change
1. Strategic leadership			
2. Goal setting			
3. Decision-making, problem-solving and action planning			
4. Effectiveness of communication			
5. Conflict management and resolution			
6. Personal and inter-group relations			
7. Relations between leaders and followers			
8. Individual learning			
9. Team learning			
10. Organisational learning			
11. Use of information Communication Technology (ICT)			

The above tool is used in the same way as the one above. The strength with this tool is that the processes are much clearer in terms of the benefits they entail as compared to the components in the first tool. But as stated earlier, it may be more effective to use both tools for complementarity and triangulation.

The assumption in using the above monitoring and evaluation tools is that the organizations and people using them have been oriented to what OD is and that they understand what the components or processes mean. In other words, they are able to differentiate between when these are 'healthy' or not. Assessing progress using the indicators must be done against the assessment results on one hand and the 'word picture or ideal picture' on the other.

In some cases, indicators like structure or effectiveness of communication may be too broad. In such cases, the people and the organization may need to think of more specific indicators under such categories. The way to go about this is ask and discuss questions like, "how can we tell if the structure is what we want it to be?" or "how can we tell if the communication is what we want it to be?"

Such indicators therefore may look like:

Structure:

- Clarity of organogram among members of staff (0 – 5)
- Clarity of individuals' roles and responsibilities (0–5)
- Clarity of departmental roles and responsibilities (0–5)

Communication:

- The level of individual's involvement in project planning (0–5)
- Amount of information shared before decisions are implemented (0–5)
- Responsiveness of leaders to suggestions from juniors (0–5)

The situation may dictate whether to use the headings as indicators or find more refined indicators under the subheadings. The key however is to enable the organization to consciously move towards its ideal situation as stipulated in the word picture.

Monitoring and evaluation enable the organization to track progress. Monitoring enables the organization to know whether it is still on track regarding its milestones along the way. Evaluations enable the organization to know whether it has achieved its goals or not. Monitoring and evaluations enable the organization to make informed decisions on the way forward.

The most important lessons in managing the OD process

It is not wise to use clutches when one can walk on their own feet
Do not scratch where it does not itch

The most important lesson in the OD process is to seek at every stage to imagine yourself in your client's shoes. This enables the OD practitioner to always genuinely be able to see situations, dynamics and problems from the client's perspectives as well as from your own (Essinger 1994: 123). This discipline of looking at situations from the client's point of view forces the OD practitioner to realize that, "your own priorities and time frames may not be your client's priorities and timeframes" (Essinger 1994: 123).

Related to the above is the need for the OD practitioner to 'assess' the stage of development of the organization and to always be aware of what really matters in general at that particular stage of development. This enables the practitioner to only 'scratch where it is itching'. The use of OD in development organizations for example has been criticized for 'forcing' organizations to 'formalize' before they are ready leading to artificial and mechanical changes. In this situation, it is important to be mindful of the fact that the aim of OD may be helping an organization to make a smooth transition to its next stage of development or to help the organization be the best it can be in its particular stage of development (if it is not 'ripe' to move to its next stage of development). What really matters for organizations that are in the first stage of development, for example, are ensuring positive leadership, managing relationships to ensure team spirit and strengthening transparency and accountability and helping them demonstrate the impact of their work. Scratching where it does not itch may alienate the owners of the organization.

Chapter Eight	Chiku Malunga
	Organizational Wisdom in 100 African Proverbs (An Introduction to Organizational Paremiology)
	London & Abuja, Adonis & Abbey Publishers

Some Lessons on Using African Proverbs from Our Practice

We have used African proverbs in OA processes, but also in strategic planning, team building, leadership development, board development and self-development interventions. We have also used African proverbs in working with a range of organizations including: community based organizations (CBOs), professional NGOs, churches and government departments. From this experience we have learnt a number of lessons, including:

In the proverbs based self-assessment tools, the proverbs act as a 'communication aid or amplifier'. The participants discuss their understanding of the proverbs. They then apply this understanding when answering the question and determining the assessment rate and its explanation (see the example above). We have also learnt that it is often necessary to use an external facilitator to moderate the discussions and the self-assessment process.

It is necessary to use the most fitting proverb to the intervention or situation at hand. Using 'loose' proverbs without a clear link to the intervention or the situation may lead to confusing the people and disrupting the process. The practitioner must always ask himself or herself the question, what is the most effective proverb that I can use in this situation?" In roles and responsibilities clarification intervention, for example, proverbs like, *if the sun says it is more powerful than the moon, then let it come and shine at night* and *the cat in his house has the teeth of a lion* may be very appropriate. In communicating the importance of learning from practice, a proverb like *a person is taller than any mountain they have climbed* would be appropriate.

In training workshops it is important to use only a few proverbs to maximize their impact. Too many proverbs may lead to loss of interest in the proverbs. This also applies to carrying out assessments using the proverbs based tools. In a three–day team building workshop, for example, we use about three proverbs in one session at the beginning of the workshop to surface issues and insights for discussion. In the proverbs-based assessment tool, this may mean that

Chapter Eight	Chiku Malunga *Organizational Wisdom in 100 African Proverbs (An Introduction to Organizational Paremiology)* London & Abuja, Adonis & Abbey Publishers

not all categories may need the proverbs - only where proverbs will add significant value. In other words, proverbs are more useful where a direct question may not surface all the insights because people do not completely understand the question or the issue.

It is important to use reflective questions in order to bring out the insights from the proverbs. Since proverbs may mean different things to different people at different times and in different contexts, the questions must be properly phrased and focused to enable them to solicit only those insights related to the issue at hand. In a self-development session, for example, we use a question like: What insights can we learn from the following proverb: *A changed place cannot transform an individual but a transformed individual can change a place.* When we used this question and proverb with a rural CBO, a chief explained his total agreement with the proverb by telling the group a story of an individual in his village who migrated to a neighboring country hoping to be 'transformed' by its better economy and somebody else who came from that country to reside in his village. The person who came to reside in his village was a very productive individual and within a short time he became very wealthy. The person who migrated to the other country came back after a few years frustrated and poorer as the 'transformed nation' failed to transform him.

Proverbs can also be used as reflective case studies. To do this more effectively, it is important to know and use the story upon which the proverbs are based. Using a story is especially useful on complicated issues, which are difficult to communicate. For example, it is extremely difficult to teach and communicate organisational identity issues. But, using 'proverbs case studies' can easily transcend such a barrier. Finally, proverbs must be used naturally and flexibly, not mechanically. If used mechanically, the proverbs may actually become a hindrance to the process. The power of proverbs when used properly is their 'invisibility' as they serve to facilitate the process rather than draw attention to themselves. This means that proverbs must be used only when their use will add value to the process. Development practitioners must not get too excited with the use of

Chapter Eight	Chiku Malunga
	Organizational Wisdom in 100 African Proverbs (An Introduction to Organizational Paremiology)
	London & Abuja, Adonis & Abbey Publishers

proverbs to the extent of *'using crutches when they can walk on their own feet'.*

Concluding Remarks

The OD process is basically a learning process built on the proverb, *the world is a school, the earth a classroom and experience, the best teacher.* OD interventions and programs are aimed at creating credible, sustainable and high impact organizations. Organizational credibility or integrity, sustainability and impact will result in the following benefits for the people the organizations serve: more physically, mentally and spiritually healthy individuals and communities; more and better job opportunities; more disposable income; and strong and healthy families with children living better lives than their parents. These benefits represent OD's contribution to development and organizational practice.

Undertaking an OD process is the way of cultivating organizational wisdom. It is a way of preparing the organization for the tomorrow it desires, for *when one is prepared difficulties do not come.* The use of African proverbs and other forms of indigenous wisdom will play a continually increasing role in the understanding and practice of Organization Development in the unfolding future.

Managing the OD Process:

1. What do the following proverbs teach us about when to call for OD interventions and processes?

To see a snail's eyes one must be patient
A fruit does not ripe in a day
A patient mouse in a young banana plant will one day eat a ripe banana
There are no short cuts to the top of the palm tree

2. How does the following proverb describe how conscious we are about our organization's need of external help in the form of consultants?

It is the sick person who calls for a doctor

3. How does the following proverb describe our experiences in working with and what we look for in an external consultant?

The dog that barks the loudest does not bite

4. What does the following proverb teach us about the importance of contracts?

Birds agree first before they fly together

5. How does the following proverb help us see the link between our organizational performance and its internal capacity?

A healthy chick comes from a healthy egg

6. What does the following proverb tell us about implementing capacity building plans?

It is not just by looking at a newly married wife that she will become pregnant

7. What does the following proverb tell us about monitoring and evaluating the implementation of our organization's capacity building plan?

The person who does not know where he is going will not realize it when he has arrived

Bibliography

Becker, E. (1996) Global Ecology and Global Society in *Development Models and Worldviews*, DSE, Frankfurt

Beckhard, R & Pritchard, W. (1992) *Changing the Essence: The Art of Creating and Leading Fundamental Change in Organizations*, Jossey-Bass Publishers, San Francisco.

Bentley, T. (1998) *Learning Beyond the Class Room: Education for a Changing World*, Rutledge, London.

Blunt, P & Jones, M. (1992) *Managing Organizations in Africa*, De Gruyter Studies in Organization, Berlin.

Buber, M. 1937. *I and Thou*. T & T Clark, Edinburgh

Cole, G. (1997) Personnel Management: Theory and Practice, Continuum, London.

Commission for Africa, (2005): 'Our Common Interest: Report of the Commission for Africa', March

Conger, J. (1989) *The Charismatic Leader: Behind the Mystique of Exceptional Leadership*, Jossey-Bass Publishers, San Franscisco

Covey, S. 2004. *The 8th Habit: From Effectiveness to Greatness*, Simon & Schuter, London

Dainty, P & Anderson, M. (1996) *The Capable Executive: Effective Performance in Senior Management*, Macmillan Press Ltd, London.

Drucker, P. (1955) *Managing for Results*, Butterworth-Heinemann, Oxford.

Drucker, P. (1967) *The Effective Executive*, Butterworth-Heinemann, Oxford.

Drucker, P. (1990) *Managing the Non-Profit Organization*, Butterworth-Heinemann, Oxford.

Drucker, P. (1991) *Managing for the Future*, Butterworth-Heinemann, Oxford.

Drucker, P. (1974) *Management: Tasks, Responsibilities, Practices*, Butterworth-Heinemann, Oxford.

Drucker, P. (1980) *Managing in Turbulent Times*, Butterworth-Heinemann, Oxford.

Dunphy, D. (1981) *Organisational Change by Choice*, McGraw – Hill Book Company, Auckland.

Edersheim, E. 2007. *The Definitive Drucker*, MCGraw-Hill: New York

Essinger, J. (1994) *Starting a High – Income Consultancy*, Pitman Publishing, London

Fowler, A. (1996) *Institutional Development and NGOs in Africa: Policy Perceptions for European Development Agencies*, INTRAC, Oxford.

French, W & Bell Jnr, C. (1995) *Organization Development: Behavioral Science Interventions for Organization Improvement* (5th edition), Prentice-Hall Inc, New Jersey.

Grundy, T. (1993) *Implementing Strategic Change: A Practical Side for Business*, Kogan Page Ltd, London.

Hammer, M & Champy, J (2001) *Reengineering the Corporation*, Nicholas Brealey Publishing, London

Hammer, M. 2003. *Agenda: What Every Business Must Do to Dominate the Decade*, Three Rivers Press: New York.

Handy, C. (1985) *Understanding Organizations*, Penguin Group, London.

Handy, C. (1998) *Understanding Voluntary Organizations*, Penguin, Harmmondsworth.

Hanson, P & Lubin, B. (1995) *Answers to Questions Most Frequently Asked About Organization Development*, Sage Publications, London.

Harvard Business School, 2006. *Classic Drucker*, Harvard Business School Publishing Corporation: Boston.

Herman, S. (2001) Notes on OD for the 21st Century Organization in *Organization Development Journal Vol 19 No 1*.

Holloway, R. (1997) *Exit Strategies: Transition from International to Local NGO Leadership*, PACT Washington DC.

Howell, W. (1976) *Essentials of Industrial and Organisational Psychology*, the Dorsey Press, Homewood, Illinois.

Jackson, D. (1997) *Dynamic Organizations: The Challenge of Change*, Macmillan Press Ltd, London.

Jackson, T. (2002) *Theories in Management and Change in Africa*. www.Africamgt.org

James, R. (1998) *Demystifying Organization Development: Practical Capacity Building Experience of African NGOs*, INTRAC, Oxford.

James, R. (2002) *People and Change: Exploring Capacity Building in NGOs*, INTRAC, Oxford.

James, R. (2003) *Leaders Changing Inside-Out: What Causes Leaders to Change Behaviour? Cases from Malawian Civil Society.* The International NGO Training and Research Centre INTRAC Occasional Papers Series No: 43

Johnson, H & Wilson, G (1999) Institutional Sustainability as Learning in *Development in Practice Vol 9 no 1 & 2.*

Jones, M and Blunt, P. (1993) Organization Development and Change in *Africa in Africa in International Journal of Public Administration 16 (11), 1735 –1765.*

Kaplan, A. (1996) *The Development Practitioners' Handbook*, Pluto Press, London.

Kniglanski, W (1975) Conflict and Power. In P.G Swingle (Ed), *The Structure of Conflict* (pp. 177 – 219). New York: Academic Press

Kumakanga, S. (1975) *Nzeru za Kale (Wisdom of Ancient Times)*, Longman, Blantyre.

Livegoed, B. (1969) *Managing the Developing Organization*, Blackwell, Oxford.

Livegoed, B. (1973) *The Developing Organization*, Tavistock, London.

Lynch, J. (1995) *Customer Loyalty and Success*, Macmillan Press Ltd, London.

Maathai, W. (1995) *Bottlenecks of Development in Africa*, United Nations Centre for Human Settlement (Habitat).

Malunga, C (2004) *Understanding Organizational Sustainability through African Proverbs*. Impact Alliance. Washington D.C

Malunga, C. (2000) The Beehive Model for Team Building, Paper Published in *Footsteps Magazine no 4.*

Mandela, N. (1994) *Long Walk to Freedom*, Little, Brown and Co. London

Maxwell, J. (1998) *The 21 Irrefutable Laws of Leadership*, African Nazarine Publications, Florida, RSA.

Mbeki, T. (1998) *The African Renaissance: South Africa and the World*, the United Nations University, Tokyo.

Mbigi, L. (1995) *Ubuntu – The Spirit of African Transformation Management*, Knowledge Resource, Randburg.

Megginson, D & Peddler, M. (1992) *Self-Development: A Facilitator's Guide*, McGraw-Hill Book Company, Berkshire.

Molotlegi, K. (2004). Indigenous Leadership for Progressing Africa: Paper Presented on 12th October 2004 in Addis Ababa, Ethiopia

Morgan, G. (1989) *Images of Organization,*Sage Publications, London.

Mulle, H. (2001) Challenges to African Governance and Civil Society in *Public Administration and Development Vol 21 pp 71 – 76*.

Munroe, M (1996) *Maximizing Your Potential: The Keys to Dying Empty*, Destiny Image Publishers, Inc, Shippensburg.

Murithi, T. n.d. *Practical Peace Making Wisdom from Africa: Reflections on Ubuntu*, www.bath,ac.uk

Nabi, I & Luthria, M. (eds) (2002) *Building Competitive Firms: Incentives and Capabilities*, The World Bank, Washington, D.C.

Nangoli, M, (1986*) No More Lies about Africa: Here's the Truth from an African*, Heritage Publishers, New Jersey.

Natemeyer, W (1979) *Situational Leadership, Perception, and the Impact of Power*. Escondido, CA: Leadership Studies

Nee, W (1977) *The Spiritual Man, Christian Fellowship Publishers*, Inc New York

Olive Subscription Service, (1997) *How Well Do You Read Your Organization? Ideas for a Change*, Olive Publications, Durban

Orwell, G (1945) *Animal Farm*, Penguin, London

Orwell, G (1949) *Nineteen Eighty Four*, Penguin, London

Parker, M. (1990) Team *Players and Team Work: The New Competitive Business Strategy*, San Fransisco: Jossey –Bass.

Porter, L & Tanner, S. (1998) *Assessing Business Excellence*, Butterworth-Heinemann, Oxford.

Raven, B (1959) The Bases of Social Power. In D. Cartwright (Ed), *Studies in Social Power* (pp. 15 – 167). Ann Arbor, MI: Institute for Social Research, University of Michigan.

Chapter Eight	Chiku Malunga
	Organizational Wisdom in 100 African Proverbs (An Introduction to Organizational Paremiology)
	London & Abuja, Adonis & Abbey Publishers

Sahley, C. (1995) *Strengthening the Capacity of NGOs: Cases of Small Enterprises Development in Africa*, INTRAC, Oxford.

Sampson, A. (1999) *Mandela: The Authorized Biography*, Harper Collins Publishers, London.

Senge, P. (1990) *The Fifth Discipline: The Art and Practice of the Learning Organization*, Double Day, New York

Senge, P., Scharmer, C., Jaworski, J & Flowers, B. 2004. *Presence: Human Purpose and the Field of the Future*, Society for Organisational Learning, Inc, Cambridge, MA

Smillie, I & Hailley, J. (2001) *Managing for Change: Leadership, Strategy and Management in Asian NGOs*, Earth scan Publications Ltd, London

Stewart, D. 2005. *Wisdom from Africa: A Collection of Proverbs*, Struik Publishers, Cape Town

Tandon, R (1996) *Understanding Design of Organization*, PRIA, New Delhi, WA: Kola Tree Pr

Tangwa, G. (1998) Democracy and Development in Africa: Putting the Horse before the Cart. Road Companion to Democracy and Meritocracy, Bellington, WA: Kola Tree Press

Tengey, W. (1991) *A Guide to Promote Rural Self-Reliant Development (a Ghana Experience)*, Africa Centre for Human Development, Accra

Thaw, D. (1999), *Developing Policy for Organizations: An Organic Process*, Olive Publications, Durban

Tutu, D. (1999), *No Future Without Forgiveness.* London: Rider Books.

Vincent, F. (1995) *Alternative Financing of Third World Development Organizations and NGOs*, IRED, Geneva

Waiguchu, J. (2001) *Management of Organizations in Africa: A Handbook and Reference*, Quorum Books, London

Williams, A. 2002. On the Subject of Kings and Queens: "Indigenous African Leadership and the Diasporal Imagination". African Studies Quarterly/ www.africa.uf/.edu/asq/v7:a4.htm

APPENDIX 1:

African Proverbs Organizational Self-Assessment Tool

Rating (0–5): 0 = We do not experience this in our organization
5 = We strongly experience or observe this in our organization

CATEGORY AND 'REFLECTION' PROVERBS	RATING (0–5)	EXPLANATION
1. Culture		
a) *How conscious are the people of the effect of their behaviours and attitudes on the effectiveness of the organization?* • The owner of a smell does not notice it • You cannot tell the quality of a fig fruit by its outside appearance		
b) *How clear is the identity of the organization both to insiders and other stakeholders?* • Because of his double identity, the bat was never buried		
c) *How free are people to express their real feelings in this organization?* • When hunting animals will only come out when you make noise/ the man who kicks his old friend for warning him that the path he has chosen is disastrous can only		

be headed for trouble		
d) *How are people judged in this organization/ what is given value?* • Do not be quick to insult the mad man who frequently comes at your home's door steps, he may become your mother's husband		
e) *How transparent are processes and the way decisions are made in this organization* f) *You can't hide the smoke when the house is burning*		
g) *How well does the organization balance action and learning?* h) *When the lion runs and looks back, it's not that he is afraid, rather he is trying to see the distance he has covered*		
i) *How Committed are Employees to stay on in this Organization?* • A bird in hand is worthy than two in the bush • Grass may be greener on the other side but it is just as difficult to cut		
j) *How well does the organization do in terms of trying to create an empowering organisational culture?* • Constructive arguments build a village • A visitor brings a sharper razor blade		

2.	**Leadership and Vision**		
a)	*How clear and well shared is the vision of the organization* • What the eyes have seen the heart cannot forget • You can only jump over a ditch if you have seen it from a far		
b)	*How Effective is the Leadership Role in this Organization?* • An army of sheep led by a lion would defeat an army of lions led by a sheep • When kings lose direction they become servants		
c)	*How do the leadership styles being practiced in this organization meet the different leadership needs of the organization?* • When the beat of the drum changes, so must the step of the dance		
d)	*How well does the organization develop its leadership for current and future needs in the areas of:* *Effective Time Management* • Time never goes back *Concentrating and focusing on high leverage efforts and activities* • At the cross road you cannot go in both directions at the		

same time *Leadership Succession* • When a reed dries up, another one grows in its place *Building Integrity* • A crab's daughters cannot walk differently from their mother • Character is like pregnancy, you cannot hide it for long *Widening Personal and Organisational Exposure* • To him who has never traveled a small garden is a big forest • The eyes that have seen an ocean cannot be satisfied by a mere lagoon • A bird that has flown over a sea cannot be afraid of a river		
3. Strategy		
a) How well is the organization using its 'cutting edge' against competition? • A mother of twins must sleep on her back		
b) How well does the leadership balance long-term and short-term needs in their thinking and planning in this organization?		

• Since men have learnt to shoot without missing, birds have learnt to fly without perching • There is no such a thing as bad weather, only bad clothing		
c) How consciously and proactively does the organization learn from what is happening in its task environment? • If you can bear the hissing of a snake do not complain when you are bitten		
d) How conscious are people in the organization about the changes in the state of the internal health of the organization over time? • An egg does not go bad in one day		
e) In addressing its issues, it is the organization addressing real issues or only symptoms? • If you cut a piece of a liana creeper without removing the roots, it will continue to creep		
f) How Effective are the Strategies the Organization is Implementing in terms of: *Identifying and Utilizing Leverage* • A hunter with one arrow does not shoot a careless aim • If you are not pretty know		

how to sing *Being focused for Concentration* • When you are at the crossroad you cannot go in both directions at the same time *Being realistic about the organization's capacity to carry out its work* • What a duck has failed to pick, a chicken cannot *Recognizing that Organisational Growth and Development takes Time* • There are no short cuts to the top of a palm tree • Even the biggest cock that crows the loudest was once upon a time just an egg • Little by little the snail reached its destination **Implementing Strategies** • A lazy man's farm is the breeding ground for snakes • Pray for a good harvest, but keep on hoeing • Success is a ladder which cannot be climbed with hands in your pocket		

4. Roles and Responsibilities

a) How Well are the Roles and Responsibilities Defined and Respected in this Organization?		

• Two cocks do not crow in the same pen(check this word 'pen') • Two fingers cannot enter into one nostril • A cat in his house has the teeth of a lion • If the sun says it is more powerful than the moon, then let it come and shine at night		
b) How Well is Conflict Managed in this Organization? • You cannot kill the rat when it is sitting on your clay pot • There is no venom like that of the tongue • When elephants fight it is the grass that suffers		
c) How Strong is the Team Spirit in this Organization? • No matter how powerful a man, he cannot make rain fall on his farm only • One person cannot move a mountain • Friendship is adding value • The man who eats alone dies alone • United we are rock and divided we are sand		
d) How well do individuals and departments work together and how well does the organization work		

	together with other organizations? k) When cobwebs unite, they can tie up a lion		
e)	*How Well are Power and Politics Exercised in the Organization?* l) Those who live in peace work for it m) We make war so that we can live in peace n) Negotiate with your enemy whilst you are a strong and formidable force, and he will always fear and respect you; but negotiate at the brink of defeat, and he will trample you down		
5.	**Policies, Systems and Procedures**		
a)	*How Effective are the Rules and Regulations in the Organization?* o) Rules are stronger than an individual's power p) There can be no village without rules		
b)	*How Effective is the Process of Formulating the Policies, Systems and Procedures* • A chief should not make rules alone • A chief should not make rules when he is angry		

6. **Sustainability**		
a. How Sustainable is the Organization in its Client, Organisational and Financial **Aspects?** q) Money is not everything r) Your own farm implements are more important than your mother and father s) The time to make friends is before you need them t) Recognition comes with having one's own possessions		

APPENDIX 2

A Summary of Key Organizational Characteristics at Different Phases

CATEGORY	PIONEER PHASE	INDEPENDENT PHASE	INTERDEPENDENT PHASE
1. Culture			
Consciousness of Organisational Culture	• Not conscious	• Not conscious	• Efforts taken to understand organisational culture and its effect on organisational effectiveness • The organization is values driven
Clarity of Identity of the	• Organizational identity	• Identity not clear	• Identity tied up in what the

Organization	tied up in the personality of the leader		organization does, the organization has a distinct and positive image
Types of Organisation-al Culture	• 'following' culture, dissent is punished	• People are inward focused • Secrecy and limited sharing of information • Much action without reflection and learning • Alienation and fantasy	• Alternative views are encouraged • People are outward, contribution and service focused • Openness and sharing of information encouraged • People find meaning in their work and organizations
2. Leadership			
Clarity of Vision	• Clear and strong vision with the leader or a few individuals but not widely shared	• Vision blurred	• Clear, strong, inspiring and shared vision among the people in the organization and all stakeholders
Leadership Effectiveness	• Charismatic leadership • Leaders biased towards participatory tendencies, the future and being proactive in response to	• More management as compared to leadership • Leaders biased towards autocratic tendencies, the past and reacting	• Leadership and management balanced • Leaders balancing the needs of the present and the future, participatory and autocratic tendencies and being proactive

Chapter Eight — Chiku Malunga
Organizational Wisdom in 100 African Proverbs (An Introduction to Organizational Paremiology)
London & Abuja, Adonis & Abbey Publishers

	opportunities in the environment	to environmental challenges	and reactive
Developing Leadership	• Leadership development not given priority	• Leadership development given attention but on a superficial level, more attention given to management development	• Leadership development given serious attention. This is done among others through: • Improving time management • Concentration of leaders' efforts on high leverage efforts • Leadership succession planning • Improving exposure • Building integrity among the leaders
3. Strategy			
Strategic Plan	• No documented strategic plan	• Strategic plan present but mostly reactive in nature	• Strategic plan present and mostly proactive in nature
Strategic Planning Process	• If it is done at all it is usually done as a fad	• Done but not very participatory	• Wide consultations in the process and tackles 'real' issues
Effectiveness of Strategy	• The organization does not use its resources effectively and	• The organization does not use its resources efficiently	• The strategic plan is consciously implemented and the organization uses its resources efficiently and effectively

	efficiently		
4. Organisational Structure			
Organogram	• There is no clear recognized structure in the organization. The leader acts as a hub to which everyone is attached	• The organization is hierarchical	• The organization is 'flat' and people work mostly through teams. It is an organization of 'equals'. • The organization is responsive to the changing needs in the environment and has the capacity to re-organize and renew itself
Roles and Responsibilities	• Roles and responsibilities among individuals and departments are not clear	• Clear roles and responsibilities • Roles and responsibilities are fixed according to one's specialization • Individuals and departments work independently	• Redefined and clear roles and responsibilities • Roles and responsibilities are temporary and may change from time to time • Individuals and departments collaborate • Problems are solved by task forces composed of diverse professional skills • The primary commitment of the individual is to the profession rather than

			the organization • Leaders and managers work mainly as coordinators between various temporary work teams. • The organization collaborates effectively with other stakeholders
Relationships	• There is a 'family' feeling in the organization	• Relationships are 'formal'	• There are team building efforts to ensure close and satisfying relationships
5. Policies, Systems and Procedures			
Monitoring and Evaluation	• Activities are not consciously monitored and evaluated	• Activities are monitored and evaluated but in a difficult and complicated way	• Activities are monitored and evaluated in a 'user friendly way'
Human Resources	• There are no formal employment procedures • There are no clearly defined recruitment processes • There are no grievance procedures • The organization	• There are formal employment procedures • There are clearly defined recruitment processes • Grievance procedures are in place • Performance appraisals are	• Employment procedures are ethically followed • Recruitment processes are flexible but ethical • Grievance procedures are actually uses • Staff undergo 'facilitated' self-appraisal • Staff development

	does not conduct staff performance appraisals • There is no staff development plan • There are no formal procedures for salaries and benefits	conducted • Staff development plans are in place • There are formal procedures for salaries and benefits	plans are consciously implemented and adhered to • Procedures for benefits and salaries are perceived to be fair by staff
Administration	• There are no administration procedures or manuals • The procedures are informal and there is no common understanding among the staff on the procedures	• Administration procedures are formalized and functional • Administrative manuals exist but they are not fully used • Staff experience the procedures as being restrictive	• There are 'lean' administrative procedures and manuals • The procedures and manuals are adhered to • The procedures and manuals are updated regularly
Finance	• Financial procedures are incomplete • Operating funds are not separated according to project • Budgets are not adequate and they are not used as management	• The organization's operating funds are separated to avoid cross project financing • Financial procedures and reporting systems are in place and they function	• There is conscious integration of the budget into its annual plans • There is a separate unit to look into finances • There are less diversions from the budget projections

	tools • There are no procedures for handling procurement and stock control • There are no audits and external financial reviews • There is no system to report on the organizations financial status • Financial reports are not consciously used in planning and reviewing progress • The organization has limited sources of finances and lacks capacity to diversify sources of finances	'partially' • Budget projections and expenditures often do not match • The organization has more than one source of finance • The organization has skills to diversify the sources of its finances	• Procurement and stock control systems are in place and being effectively used • External audits are conducted on a regular basis • Registered firms of auditors prepare financial reports. They are published and disseminated • The report contains balance sheets and attachments • The board reviews the financial report and endorses it • The report is consciously used in planning and review • The organization has multiple sources of finances • The organization has an effective financial strategy
Information and Communica-tion Systems	• The organization does not have a 'conscious' system to collect, analyze and disseminate data • Information is	• There is an operational information system that most staff have access to • The information	• The organization has trained personnel to manage its information systems • The system enables the organization to process, disseminate

	not systematically collected and is often done manually • The collected information is not shared among stakeholders	collected is not fully and effectively used • The information is not consciously linked to the organization's planning process • The organization lacks mechanisms to solicit feedback	and get feedback on the information

6. Sustainability

Client Sustainability	• The actual and potential clients do not feel a special attachment to the services or product of the organization • The organization has some idea about how to meet the needs of its target groups • The organization has no track record	• The actual and potential clients recognize the benefits of the services or products of the organization • The organization has established some mutual relationships with its clients • The organization is able to deliver effective and appropriate services and products	• The organization's services and products are supported by the clients • The clients feel a special attachment to the services and products of the organization • The organization has developed a system of involving the clients in service and product definition and delivery • The organization has identified and established its niche in the market
Organizational Sustainabil	• The organization does not have	• The organization 'forgets' its purpose and staff look at the	• The organization has a shared vision of its role in society

ity	a shared vision and skills to effectively involve staff and stakeholders • The organization is not involved in coalitions and networks	organization mostly as a means of making a living • The organization may be involved in coalitions and networks but does not fully benefit from these	• The organization has capacity to reorganize itself in response to present and anticipated changes in the task environment • The organization contributes to the development of an enabling environment for organizations to thrive in
Financial Sustainability	• The organization has limited sources of finances • The organization does not have a financial strategy • The organization's finances are insufficient to meet its plans	• The organization explores different sources of finance • The organization is not very successful against its competitors	• The organization has a diversified financial base • The organization has an effective financial strategy • The organization is successful against its competitors • The organization is mostly self-supporting

Index

A

Akpan, Otoabasi, Ii
American Association For The Advancement Of Science (AAAS), 10

B

Baobab Tree, 61, 86, 102, 107, 122, 146, 147, 158
Bureaucratic Institutions, 87
Big Picture Consciousness, 136
Bryant, Coraile, 16

C

CADECO, 38, 174
Calabash, 126
Complexity Model', 45, 48
Charcoal Fire, 162
Charismatic Leadership, 199
Columbia State University, 16
Communication System, 152, 153
Community Based Organizations, 181
Competent Local Consultants, 167
Conscious Organizational Learning, 147

D

Destructive Tension, 155
Developmental Counselling, 76, 77, 150
Dinosaurs, 105
Drucker, Peter, 32, 81, 100

E

Eastern Religious Practices, 81
Environmental Influences, 69
Einstein, Albert, 22
Ethical Entertainment, 166
Evaluation Phases, 162

F

Facilitated Self-Appraisal, 202
Feelings Of Alienation, 87
Flattening Management Structures, 43
Frankl, Victor, 69
Freelance Consultants, 166

G

Globalization, Vii, 142
Greener Pastures, 21, 71
Grid Organisation Development, 53

H

Hammer, Michael, 17, 18
Harmonious Relationships, 85
Healthy Organizational Relationships, 85
Higher Equilibrium, 37
Hypochondria, 70
HIV/AIDS, 10, 171
Human Rights Centre (HRC), 50, 170

I

Industry Specific Factors, 113
Internal Health', 56
Information, Communication, Technology, 30

Internal Scanning, 114
Intervention Planning, 26

J

Joint Prioritization, 169

K

Kenyatta, Jomo, 56

L

Legitimacy, 20
Legal Structure, 129

M

Marley, Bob, 109, 162
Mazive, Alfredo, 161, 162
Magnetic Personalities, 90
Mechanistic Organization, 87

N

Nairobi, 56
Natural Sequencing, 125
Negative Organizational Politics, 86, 102

O

Organisational Capacity, 119
Organization's Uniqueness, 108
Organizational Assessments, 17, 28, 31, 37, 51, 54, 55, 56, 57, 58, 59
Organization Development, 12, 14, 15, 16, 17, 19, 20, 34, 67, 80, 183, 186, 187

Organizational Paremiology, I, Iii, Vii, 12, 14, 15, 17, 18, 19
Organizational Procedures, I, Iii, Iv, Vii, 9, 12, 14, 15, 16, 17, 18, 19, 22, 30, 38, 39, 40, 44, 46, 47, 51, 54, 59, 62, 70, 71, 97, 112, 125, 126, 129, 137, 139, 140, 148, 157, 161, 169, 183, 187, 198, 205
Orwell, George, 96

P

Performance Forecasting, 145
Power Shift, 42
Program Accountability, 145
Process Management, 31

R

Relationships Development, 85
Restrictive Policies, 99
Rotating Directorship, 130

S

Self-Development, 62, 68, 73, 81
Singapore, 23
Social Responsibility, 116
Spiritual Dimensions, 68
Strategic Capacity, 108
Strategic Leadership, 30

T

The Agenda, 17
Threatening Environment, 74, 76
Transcendental Meditation, 81

U

University Of Malawi, 10

Index | Chiku Malunga
Organizational Wisdom in 100 African Proverbs (An Introduction to Organizational Paremiology)
London & Abuja, Adonis & Abbey Publishers

www.ingramcontent.com/pod-product-compliance
Lightning Source LLC
Chambersburg PA
CBHW022008160426
43197CB00007B/332